DOWN HOME

TEXAS
COOKING

DOWN HOME
TEXAS
COOKING

REVISED EDITION

JAMES STROMAN

TAYLOR TRADE PUBLISHING

Lanham • New York • Dallas • Boulder • Toronto • Oxford

Published by Taylor Trade Publishing
An imprint of The Rowman & Littlefield Publishing Group, Inc.
4501 Forbes Boulevard, Suite 200
Lanham, Maryland 20706

Distributed by National Book Network

Library of Congress Cataloging-in-Publication Data

Stroman, James.
  Down home Texas cooking / James Stroman.—2nd ed.
    p. cm.
  Includes index.
  ISBN 1-58979-100-2 (pbk. : alk. paper)
  1. Cookery, American—Southwestern style. 2. Cookery—Texas.
I. Title.
TX715.2.S69S75 2004
641.59764—dc22   2004002845

℞ ™ The paper used in this publication meets the minimum requirements of
American National Standard for Information Sciences—Permanence of Paper
for Printed Library Materials, ANSI/NISO Z39.48–1992.
Manufactured in the United States of America.

CONTENTS

INTRODUCTION

The stars at night
Are big and bright,
Deep in the heart of Texas. . . .

AND SO IS the abundance of great and hearty foods. Texas is definitely a land of contrasts and its food is no exception. Just name your favorite and you'll find it—somewhere between Amarillo in the western panhandle and Texarkana on the Arkansas border, from the Red River and Oklahoma in the north all the way south to the Gulf and old Mexico, or from the grand state of Louisiana west to the vast spaces of New Mexico.

I have traveled these borders and have partaken of such delicacies as salt-rising bread, bourbon cake, oysters broiled with bacon, palate-tingling hard and soft pralines, porcupine pudding, Creole eggs, macaroon ice cream, polenta, arroz con pollo, green chile enchiladas, tamale pie, apricot and pineapple conserve atop piping-hot buttered biscuits, molasses custard, chicken barbecued in cabbage, duck in green mole, pheasants with paprika, calico coleslaw, shrimp rarebit, crab español, fish and cheese casserole, jambalaya Lafitte, redfish piquant, cream of avocado soup, senegalese, sweet and sour green beans. . . .

And like oil derricks and grazing cattle, Mexican food is an indigenous Texas reality. It isn't really the Mexican cuisine so often prepared in the parts of the state adjoining Mexico, but a hybrid called Tex-Mex. Because of the countless Mexican-Americans who settled Texas and brought their favorite foods with them, these Tex-Mex dishes have been acculturated into Texas life. They include splendid offerings like tortillas—thin Mexican bread made of ground corn and water; tostados—tortillas cooked until crisp and served with a dip called salsa picante made from pungent chile peppers; tacos—crisp-fried, folded tortillas filled with cheese, meat, lettuce, and tomatoes; bunellos—thin, crisp delicacies spread with sugar and cinnamon; tamales—meat packed within a corn batter; nachos—crisp tortillas covered with delicious melted cheeses and jalapeno peppers; and enchiladas of all descriptions, from those served with authentic Mexican mole sauce to the Tex-Mex variety containing onions, cheese, and chile con carne.

The recipes for these and many more Texas-style dishes are here in plain, everyday Texas verbiage. So move on over to your Magic Chef or campfire and treat yourself to a genuine Texas meal.

Texas has changed a lot since I first wrote this book. It's indeed a land of contrasts, with wide-open spaces and densely populated metropolitan areas. As I've continued to travel the state and sample its food, I've tasted the change. When my publisher asked me to update this book, I used the opportunity to add some great new Texas recipes and revise some older classics. I'm sure you'll find the new mix to be a tasty extravaganza.

Enjoy!

James Stroman

BEFORE WE START . . .

TABLE OF EQUIVALENTS

BUTTER

2 c = 1 lb
½ oz = 1 tbsp

CHEESE

4 c, grated = 1 lb

CHOCOLATE

1 sq = 1 oz

COCOA

4 c = 1 lb
If substituted for 1 oz chocolate,
use 3 tbsp cocoa and 1 tbsp fat

COFFEE

5½ c = 1 lb

CORNSTARCH

1 tbsp = 2 tbsp flour for thickening

DATES, PITTED

10 oz = 2 c chopped

EGG WHITES

8 large = 1 c

FLOUR, UNSIFTED

3½ c = 1 lb

MARSHMALLOWS

16 large = ½ lb

MILK

1 c = ½ c evaporated milk and ½ c water

RICE

1 c raw = 3–4 c, cooked

SUGAR

Brown
  2¼ c, firmly packed = 1 lb
Powdered
  3½ c, sifted = 1 lb
Granulated
  2¼ c = 1 lb

TABLE OF WEIGHTS AND MEASURE

3 teaspoons = 1 tablespoon
½ fluid ounce = 1 tablespoon
16 tablespoons = 1 cup
8 fluid ounces = 1 cup
½ pint = 1 cup
16 fluid ounces = 2 cups

1 pint = 2 cups
1 ounce = 28 grams
1 pound = 483 grams
1 pint = ½ liter
1 quart = 1 liter

AVERAGE CAN SIZE

Can size	Weight	Cups
No. ½	8 oz	1
No. 1	10½ oz	1¼
No. 2	20 oz	2½
No. 3	46 oz	5¾
No. 10	106 oz	13

OVEN TEMPERATURE

Slow oven	250°–325°F
Moderate oven	325°–375°F
Quick or hot oven	400°–450°F
Very hot oven	450°–550°F

DEEP-FAT FRYING

	Temperature	Time
Doughnuts, fritters, and other raw dough mixtures	370°F	3–5 minutes
Croquettes and other cooked mixtures	390°F	1–2 minutes
Potatoes, new	390°–395°F	4–8 minutes

SUGGESTIONS

Rinse bowl and beaters used for egg mixtures in cold water before washing. Hot water sets the egg and makes it difficult to remove.

When eggs are to be beaten, remove them from the refrigerator some time before using, as they beat up lighter and more quickly when not too cold.

When white sauce or gravy turns out lumpy, beat with an egg beater. If this fails, put it through a fine sieve.

Place biscuits or rolls one inch apart if you like them crusty on all sides, and touching if you like them soft.

It is easier to remove pinfeathers from a dry bird than it is from a wet, chilled one.

Save dishes by sifting or measuring dry ingredients onto waxed paper instead of into a bowl.

If muffins get done a little before the rest of the meal, loosen them and tip them slightly in the pan. Otherwise they may steam and get soggy on the bottom.

To test candy temperature, drop a little boiling syrup into a cup of cold water. If the syrup can be gathered into a soft ball, it has reached 240°F.

To help prevent leftover avocado from darkening, keep it wrapped in waxed paper with the pit until used.

To keep parsley fresh extra long, rinse it in cold water and place it in a tightly closed jar in the refrigerator.

To blanch almonds, pour boiling water over them and let them stand until their skins loosen. You can pull them off them easily.

Put a tablespoon of butter in the water when cooking macaroni or spaghetti to keep it from boiling over.

To prevent homemade mayonnaise from separating, add 1 tablespoon of hot water to each pint immediately after making.

Add cream instead of milk to canned soups to make them especially rich and delicious.

If brown sugar gets hard, place a damp cloth in the jar with the sugar and cover lightly. Storing in the refrigerator helps, too.

When cutting marshmallows, it helps to dip the scissors in hot water occasionally.

One teaspoon of double-acting baking powder to one cup of flour is the correct proportion for cakes, biscuits, and quick breads.

When measuring shortening, use the measuring cup and cold water method. If ⅓ cup of shortening is required, fill the cup ⅔ full of water and drop shortening into water until it rises to the one cup mark. Pour out water; the correct amount of shortening remains.

Brush molds for gelatin mixtures with salad oil before using. Invert for a few minutes to drain thoroughly. After gelatin has been added and is set, loosen edges with a knife, turn upside down, and shake gently. Gelatin will slide out easily without melting.

To peel oranges and grapefruit and entirely free the fruit from membranous pulp, first place fruit in hot water for five minutes. You will then be able to peel every particle of outside pulp.

To make melon balls without a melon baller, use the teaspoon or half teaspoon in your measuring-spoon set.

To peel tomatoes easily, dip them in boiling water for one minute, peel them, and cut out stem end; or hold tomato on a fork over heat until skin wrinkles and splits. Then peel and chill.

A few drops of lemon juice in the food processor before chopping sticky dates, raisins, or figs make it easier to clean.

Let croquettes stand in a warm place for half an hour before frying. They will absorb less grease than when ice cold.

CANAPÉS AND
HORS D'OEUVRES

SUGGESTIONS FOR QUICK
AND EASY HORS D'OEUVRES

1. Hollow out tiny pickled beets and stuff with caviar.
2. Combine mashed liverwurst with one-third as much chutney. Spread on thinly sliced buttered bread. Roll, chill, then toast under broiler flame.
3. Place a clove of garlic in melted butter until flavor is absorbed. Pour over crisp popcorn.
4. Toast bread on one side and spread other side with a mayonnaise and minced onion mixture. Sprinkle with grated cheese and melt under broiler flame.
5. Wrap both a cooked chicken liver and a chestnut in bacon, fasten with a toothpick, and broil until bacon is crisp.
6. Sprinkle potato or corn chips with Parmesan cheese and heat in a moderate oven.
7. Marinate artichoke hearts in garlic-seasoned French dressing and serve on toothpicks.

CHILE CON QUESO

4	LARGE ONIONS, CHOPPED	1½	TBSP SALT
3	LARGE GREEN PEPPERS, CHOPPED	1½	TSP PEPPER
10	TOMATOES, PEELED AND CHOPPED	2	TBSP PAPRIKA
4	TBSP SHORTENING	3	TBSP FLOUR
		3½	LBS PROCESSED CHEESE, GRATED
		2	C HOT WATER

Sauté onions, green peppers, and tomatoes in shortening over a low flame for 20 minutes, until tender but not browned. Add seasoning. Gradually blend in flour, then cheese, while stirring. As mixture thickens, pour in hot water and continue stirring and cooking for 10 minutes. Serve over toasted tortillas. Serves 30.

GUACAMOLE

2½	LBS RIPE HAAS AVOCADOS (6–8 AVOCADOS)	1	TSP TABASCO SAUCE (OR TO TASTE)
5–6	MEDIUM TOMATOES, SEEDED AND DICED	¼	C FRESH LEMON JUICE
1	C MINCED GREEN ONIONS	½	C CHOPPED FRESH CILANTRO
		1	TSP SALT (OR TO TASTE)

Halve avocados, pit, and remove flesh from skin. Mash lightly, reserving 2 pits. Combine tomatoes, green onions, Tabasco, lemon juice, cilantro, and salt; mix well. Fold tomato mixture into avocados. Place reserved pits into guacamole (this helps prevent browning), cover, and refrigerate until ready to serve. Serve with chips, jicama strips, cut vegetables, or as an accompaniment to Tex-Mex specialties. Makes 1½ quarts.

COCKTAIL RAREBIT

¼	LB AMERICAN CHEESE	¾	TSP PREPARED MUSTARD
3	TBSP MILK	½	ONION, FINELY GRATED
2½	TBSP MAYONNAISE		DASH OF CAYENNE
2	TSP WORCESTERSHIRE		OR TABASCO

G rate cheese and combine with remaining ingredients. In a double boiler, heat mixture over boiling water until melted and smooth. Serve hot with potato chips or corn chips. Serves 4.

TEXAS HORS D'OEUVRE

1	GARLIC CLOVE	MAYONNAISE
1	3-OZ PKG CREAM CHEESE	CAYENNE PEPPER
1	1-OZ CAN ANCHOVIES	SANDWICH BREAD
		BUTTER, MELTED

R ub a bowl with garlic. Mash cream cheese and drained anchovies together in the bowl. Blend in mayonnaise until mixture is spreadable. Add cayenne to taste.

Spread on thin slices of sandwich bread, from which crusts have been removed. Roll up each slice and fasten with a toothpick. Place in a damp cloth and chill until ready to use. Brush with melted butter, remove toothpicks, and toast under the broiler flame until golden brown. Filling is also good on crackers. Serves 4.

CHILI CHEESE CANAPÉ

1 LB SHARP AMERICAN
   CHEESE
1 C PECANS
1 GARLIC CLOVE,
   PEELED
1 3-OZ PKG CREAM
   CHEESE

SALT TO TASTE
DASH OF CAYENNE
   PEPPER
CHILI POWDER

Put American cheese, pecans, and garlic through a food processor, using the medium blade. Blend in cream cheese, salt, and cayenne. Form into a long roll. Sprinkle chili powder on waxed paper and roll cheese in it until well coated. Wrap in waxed paper and chill. Slice thin and serve with crackers. Makes about 3 dozen.

SHERRY SPREAD

1–2 GARLIC CLOVES
     CREAM CHEESE
     ROQUEFORT CHEESE

OLIVE OIL
SHERRY

Rub a bowl with fresh garlic. Add equal parts cream cheese and Roquefort cheese. Moisten with a little olive oil and sherry. Store covered in refrigerator. If spread is kept any length of time, add sherry occasionally to keep it moist. Serve with crackers.

CRABMEAT ON RYKRISP

1	6½-OZ CAN CRABMEAT		SALT AND PEPPER TO TASTE
¾	C MAYONNAISE	1	6-OZ BOX RYKRISPS
¼	C CHOPPED PIMIENTO	¼	C BUTTER
		1	C GRATED AMERICAN CHEESE

Combine crabmeat, mayonnaise, pimiento, salt, and pepper. Break RyKrisps in halves and spread with butter. Top with crabmeat mixture and sprinkle with cheese. Broil until cheese is melted. Serve immediately. Serves 8.

BACON AND TOMATO CANAPÉ

COOKED BACON, FINELY CRUMBLED	ONION
MAYONNAISE	TOMATO
TOAST ROUNDS	PARSLEY
	STUFFED OLIVES

Mix bacon with mayonnaise and spread on toast rounds. Place a thin slice of onion and tomato on each canapé. Sprinkle with chopped parsley and garnish with slices of stuffed olives.

CHIP DIP

1	4-OZ CAN SHRIMP, DRAINED AND RINSED	½	C MAYONNAISE
½	C BOTTLED CHILI SAUCE	¼	C CHOPPED ONION
1	8-OZ PKG CREAM CHEESE, SOFTENED	2	TSP PREPARED HORSERADISH

Blend chili sauce into cream cheese. Mix remaining ingredients except shrimp. Then add shrimp carefully. Chill until ready to serve.

HORSERADISH CANAPÉ

6	TBSP BUTTER		DASH OF SALT
¼	C PREPARED	16	MELBA TOAST
	HORSERADISH		SQUARES
1	TSP LEMON JUICE		STUFFED OLIVES

Cream butter and horseradish together. Add lemon juice and salt. Spread on small toast squares. Garnish with sliced or chopped stuffed olives. Makes 16.

SOUFFLÉ BALLS

½	C COLD WATER	½	TSP DRY MUSTARD
2	TBSP BUTTER	1	EGG WHITE, STIFFLY
⅛	TSP SALT		BEATEN
½	C SIFTED FLOUR	½	TSP BAKING POWDER
2	EGGS		VEGETABLE OIL
4	TSP GRATED		(FOR DEEP-FRYING)
	PARMESAN CHEESE		

Combine water, butter, and salt, and bring to a boil. Remove from heat and mix in flour until smooth. Add eggs one at a time, beating well after each addition. Stir in cheese and mustard. Blend baking powder into egg white and fold into mixture.

Drop batter by the half teaspoon into oil heated to 360°F. Fry, turning several times until golden brown. Drain and sprinkle with additional Parmesan cheese. Serve at once. Makes about 40 balls the size of large marbles.

BROILED OYSTERS WITH BACON

BACON	LARGE OYSTERS

Wrap slices of bacon around large oysters, fastening ends with a toothpick. Broil under hot flame, turning frequently until crisp and brown. Serve immediately.

MUSHROOMS STUFFED WITH CRABMEAT

18	LARGE WHITE MUSHROOMS	3	TBSP CHOPPED ITALIAN PARSLEY
4	TBSP OLIVE OIL	3	TBSP CHOPPED FRESH THYME
4	TBSP UNSALTED BUTTER, PLUS EXTRA FOR BASTING (OPTIONAL)	⅓	C DRIED BREADCRUMBS
			SALT AND PEPPER TO TASTE
9	TBSP MINCED ONION	⅓	C GRATED PARMESAN CHEESE
3	GARLIC CLOVES, MINCED		
½	C CRABMEAT	½	C WHITE WINE

Preheat oven to 400°F. Wash mushrooms and remove stems. Chop the stems. Heat oil in large sauté pan over high heat. Add 4 tablespoons butter; add onions and sauté until transparent. Add garlic and mushroom stems. Sauté until wilted. Add crabmeat and cook 5 minutes, stirring all ingredients. Add parsley, thyme, and breadcrumbs. Season with salt and pepper. Stir. Stuff mixture into mushroom caps and sprinkle with cheese. Place mushroom caps in shallow dish. Add white wine. Bake uncovered for 15 minutes. If desired, baste with additional butter while cooking. Remove from oven and pour off wine. Serve hot. Serves 8.

CRAWFISH DIP

1	STICK BUTTER OR MARGARINE	1	8-OZ CAN SLICED MUSHROOMS, DRAINED
1	BUNCH GREEN ONIONS, CHOPPED	1	BUNCH FRESH PARSLEY, CHOPPED
2–3	TBSP FLOUR		SALT AND PEPPER TO TASTE
1	LB FRESH CRAWFISH TAIL MEAT		
		2½	C SOUR CREAM

Melt butter and sauté green onions until tender. Stir in flour and crawfish tail meat. Add mushrooms and parsley. Season with salt and pepper. Add sour cream and stir until well blended. Simmer about 10 minutes. Serve in chafing dish with party crackers.

MEXICAN SALSA DIP

¼	C CHOPPED CARROTS	1	TSP LEMON JUICE
½	C CHOPPED RED BELL PEPPER	1	TSP CHOPPED FRESH PARSLEY
½	C CHOPPED GREEN BELL PEPPER	1	TSP CHOPPED FRESH CILANTRO
1	16-OZ CAN PEELED TOMATOES, PLUS HALF THE JUICE	1	SMALL JALAPENO PEPPER
		2	TSP OLIVE OIL

Blend all ingredients in a food processor. Chill before serving.

S O U P S

CREOLE GUMBO

1	20-OZ CAN OKRA, OR 2 C COOKED, DICED OKRA
1	LARGE ONION, CHOPPED
2	GARLIC CLOVES, CHOPPED
3	TBSP BACON DRIPPINGS
1	GREEN PEPPER, CHOPPED
1	6-OZ CAN TOMATO PASTE
½	C CRABMEAT OR COOKED SHRIMP
½	C COOKED HAM, DICED
½	PT OYSTERS WITH LIQUID
½	TBSP FLOUR
1	TSP SALT
½	TSP PEPPER
½	TSP CAYENNE PEPPER
1	TSP THYME
2	BAY LEAVES
1	TSP MINCED FRESH PARSLEY
1	THIN SLICE OF LEMON
4	C WATER
1½	C COOKED RICE

Sauté okra, onion, and garlic in bacon drippings until browned. Mix in remaining ingredients except rice. Cover and cook slowly for 2 hours. Remove bay leaves and add rice just before serving. Serves 8.

9

ICED CUCUMBER SOUP

6	MEDIUM TOMATOES	4	PEPPERCORNS
1½	C WATER	1½	TBSP FARINA
2	ONION SLICES	1	TBSP MINCED
2	BAY LEAVES		FRESH PARSLEY
2	TBSP SUGAR	½	CUCUMBER
2	TSP SALT	1	C SOUR CREAM

Peel and chop tomatoes. (Three cups of canned tomatoes may be substituted for the fresh tomatoes and water). Add water, onion, bay leaves, sugar, salt, and peppercorns. Bring to a boil, then simmer for 15 minutes. Press through a fine sieve.

Bring strained mixture to a boil again. Gradually sprinkle in farina. Cook for 2 minutes, stirring constantly. Cool, mix in parsley, and chill.

Peel the cucumber and cut in half lengthwise. Slice paper thin. Add cucumber and sour cream to soup just before serving. Sprinkle with paprika or additional minced parsley. Serves 4 to 6.

CREAM OF AVOCADO SOUP

½	DRIED CHILE PEPPER	1	C HEAVY CREAM
3	LARGE AVOCADOS		WHIPPED CREAM
2	C UNSEASONED		CAVIAR
	CHICKEN BROTH		

Crumble dried chile pepper into a mixing bowl and add the flesh of 2 large avocados. Mash all with a potato masher and force mixture through a fine sieve into the top of a double boiler; then add chicken broth. Heat, stirring constantly until it boils. Add heavy cream, mix well, cover, and heat to boiling point. Garnish with diced flesh of remaining avocado. Season and serve or garnish with whipped cream and a touch of caviar. Or serve ice cold with generous tablespoons of caviar.

DOWN HOME TURKEY SOUP

5	C TURKEY STOCK	2	CARROTS, CUT INTO
3	CELERY STALKS, CUT		1-INCH PIECES
	INTO 1-INCH PIECES	1	ONION, QUARTERED
2	LARGE POTATOES,	1	C NOODLES,
	PEELED AND		UNCOOKED
	QUARTERED	2	C COOKED AND
			CUBED TURKEY

In a 5-quart saucepan, combine first five ingredients. Over high heat, bring to boil. Reduce heat, cover and simmer for one hour. Stir in noodles and turkey meat. Simmer until noodles are done and meat is heated through. Serves 8.

OYSTER SOUP

2	C HEAVY CREAM	1	PT FRESH OYSTERS
1	ONION, MINCED OR	2	TBSP CRACKER
	GRATED		CRUMBS
1	TBSP BUTTER		
	SALT AND PEPPER		
	TO TASTE		

Heat cream with onion and butter in the top of a double boiler. Drain juice from oysters and bring it to a boil separately. Skim and add to hot cream. Season with salt and pepper. Mix in oysters 5 minutes before serving. Serve sprinkled with cracker crumbs. Serves 4.

POTATO SOUP

2	LARGE WHITE POTATOES, PEELED AND CHOPPED	2	C HEAVY CREAM
		1	TBSP BUTTER
2	LARGE ONIONS, PEELED AND CHOPPED	¾	TSP SALT
		⅛	TSP PEPPER
			FRESH PARSLEY, MINCED

Combine potatoes and onions and cover with water. Cook until mushy over low heat—do not boil. Drain. Press through a potato ricer or food mill.

Heat cream in the top of a double boiler. Mix in butter, stirring until melted. Add potato-onion mixture, salt, and pepper. Cook until well heated. Serve garnished with minced parsley. Serves 2 to 4.

CREAM OF CORN SOUP

1	SMALL ONION, MINCED		SALT AND PEPPER TO TASTE
2	TBSP BUTTER	1	RED HOT PEPPER, SEEDED AND CHOPPED
2	TBSP FLOUR		
3	C MILK		
1	20-OZ CAN CREAMED CORN	1	EGG, SLIGHTLY BEATEN
		½	C CREAM*

Sauté onion in butter for 5 minutes without browning. Blend in flour to make a paste. Add milk and stir well. Mix in corn, salt, and pepper. Cook in a double boiler for 20 minutes. Strain and cool.

Reheat after adding red pepper. If fresh red pepper is not available, use cayenne to taste. Just before serving, mix in egg that has been combined with cream. Serves 4.

*The heavier the cream, the richer the soup.

CREAMY VICHYSSOISE

2	MEDIUM LEEKS, GREEN PARTS REMOVED	1	QT CHICKEN CONSOMMÉ (CANNED MAY BE USED)
1	LARGE ONION	2	C HEAVY CREAM
4	TBSP BUTTER		FINELY CUT
3	C PEELED AND SLICED POTATOES		FRESH CHIVES

Finely mince the whites of leeks and the onion and sauté in butter. Add sliced potatoes and chicken consommé. Cook until very soft. Put through a very fine strainer and set it to boil again. Add heavy cream and let cool. Before serving add finely cut chives.

MUSHROOM SOUP

2	C MUSHROOMS	3	TBSP FLOUR
3	TBSP BUTTER	5	TBSP MILK
4	C CHICKEN BROTH		SALT AND PEPPER
2	C HEAVY CREAM		

Scrub and slice mushrooms and stems. Sauté slowly in butter for 10 to 15 minutes, or until cooked and golden.

Heat broth over boiling water. Skim off fat and add cream. Make a paste of the flour and a little milk. Stir into broth until blended. Add mushroom mixture, and salt and pepper to taste. Cook, stirring constantly, until well heated and thickened. Serves 6 to 8. Canned mushrooms may be substituted for the fresh, in which case add them and the butter to the broth-cream mixture, without sautéing.

TOMATO EMINCE

7	RIPE LARGE TOMATOES, PEELED AND CHOPPED OR GROUND	1½	TSP SALT
		¼	TSP PEPPER
		5	TBSP MAYONNAISE
1	SMALL WHITE ONION, GRATED	1	HEAPING TSP MINCED FRESH PARSLEY
		1	TSP CURRY POWDER

Mix the first four ingredients together and chill thoroughly in a freezing tray. Do not freeze. Serve in bouillon cups with 2 teaspoons of the mayonnaise mixture (the last three ingredients) on each serving.

TOMATO-CELERY SOUP

2	LARGE CELERY STALKS	2	TBSP FLOUR
1½	C WATER	1	C CHICKEN STOCK
1½	TSP SALT	1	TSP SUGAR
2	TBSP CHOPPED ONION	½	TSP BASIL
3	TBSP BUTTER	⅛	TSP PEPPER
4	LARGE TOMATOES	1	C HEAVY CREAM

Chop celery, including leaves. Place into saucepan and add water and a half teaspoon of the salt. Cover and simmer for about 15 minutes or until tender. Measure out 1 cup combined celery and celery stock, discarding the remainder.

Sauté onion quickly in butter in a heavy iron skillet until golden, stirring constantly. Slice 3 unpeeled tomatoes. Peel and cube the remaining one. Add sliced tomatoes to onion mixture, raise heat and cook for about 10 minutes or until tender. Sprinkle with flour and continue to cook while stirring, until blended.

Mix in celery and celery stock, chicken stock, the remaining 1 teaspoon salt, sugar, basil, and pepper. Cover and simmer for 5 minutes. Press through a fine sieve. Combine with cream and the cubed tomato. Reheat to just below the boiling point and serve. Serves 4 to 6.

CREAM OF TOMATO SOUP (COLD)

6–7	MEDIUM TOMATOES, CUT IN EIGHTHS	2	TBSP CHOPPED FRESH PARSLEY
1	MEDIUM ONION, SLICED	¼	TSP PEPPER
1	TSP SALT	2	C COLD MILK
2	TSP PREPARED HORSERADISH		

Heat tomatoes, onion, and salt in a double boiler over boiling water for 20 minutes. Press through sieve, discarding skins and seeds. Add prepared horseradish, parsley, and pepper. Chill thoroughly. Add cold milk and stir well. Serves 6.

COLD TOMATO SOUP

12	MEDIUM TOMATOES	⅛	TSP CELERY SALT
3	GREEN ONIONS, MINCED	6	DROPS TABASCO SAUCE
1	TSP SALT	1	TSP WORCESTERSHIRE SAUCE
⅛	TSP PEPPER		
1	TSP SUGAR	½	CELERY STALK, MINCED
⅛	TSP SWEET MARJORAM		MINCED FRESH PARSLEY
⅛	TSP THYME		
	JUICE OF 1 LEMON	¾	C SOUR CREAM
2	TSP GRATED LEMON PEEL	1	TSP CURRY POWDER

Peel tomatoes and press through a coarse sieve. Add green onions, salt, pepper, sugar, herbs, lemon juice, lemon peel, celery salt, Tabasco sauce, Worcestershire sauce, and celery. Chill for 2 hours. Garnish with minced parsley. Top each portion with sour cream blended with curry powder. Serves 6.

CRAWFISH AND CORN SOUP

3	TBSP BUTTER	1	TSP CHOPPED GARLIC
2	TBSP CHOPPED BELL PEPPER	2	TBSP CHOPPED CELERY
1	10-OZ CAN CREAMED CORN	1	LB CRAWFISH TAIL MEAT
1	10-OZ CAN WHOLE-KERNEL CORN WITH LIQUID	1	C WATER
		1	TSP TABASCO SAUCE (OR TO TASTE)
2	TBSP CHOPPED ONION	1	PT HALF-AND-HALF

Sauté vegetables in butter until tender. Add crawfish tails and cook 2 minutes. Add water and Tabasco and simmer 5 minutes. Add half-and-half and heat, but do not boil. Serves 6.

GREEN CHILE STEW

2	LBS LEAN CUBED BEEF OR PORK	4	GARLIC CLOVES, PRESSED
2–3	ONIONS, CHOPPED	3	POTATOES
1	PT HOT GREEN CHILES, CHOPPED		SALT TO TASTE

Sauté meat and onions until brown; drain out fat. Add green chiles, garlic, and potatoes. Add enough water to cover (about 2 inches). Salt to taste. Simmer until meat is tender. More water may be added if needed. Serve with flour tortillas. Serves 4 to 6.

RHODE ISLAND CLAM CHOWDER

½	C DICED ONION	¼	C BUTTER
½	C DICED CELERY	½	C FLOUR
2	TBSP BUTTER	1	C MILK
1	8-OZ CAN CLAMS, CHOPPED (RESERVE LIQUID)	1	C HALF-AND-HALF OR HEAVY CREAM
3	C CHICKEN STOCK		DASH THYME
1	C CLAM JUICE		DASH SALT
1	C PEELED, COARSELY CHOPPED POTATOES		DASH WHITE PEPPER

In 3-quart saucepan, sauté onion and celery in 2 tablespoons butter until transparent. Add liquid from clams, chicken stock, clam juice, and potatoes. Simmer until potatoes are tender. In separate pan, melt ¼ cup butter. Stir in flour. Mix until smooth. Do not brown. Gently stir flour mixture into soup. Add clams, milk, and half-and-half or cream. Stir gently until thickened. Add seasonings. Stir and serve. Serves 4 to 6.

VEGETABLE SOUP

¼	C PEAS, SHELLED	1	OXTAIL, CUT IN SECTIONS
¼	C FRESH GREEN BEANS	1	12-OZ CAN CORN
2	MEDIUM CARROTS	1	20-OZ CAN TOMATOES
¼	C DRY LIMA BEANS	1	TBSP BARLEY
⅓	GREEN BELL PEPPER	1	TBSP RICE
1	CELERY STALK	4	CLOVES
1	LARGE ONION		SALT AND PEPPER TO TASTE
	SPRIG OF PARSLEY	1	TSP TAPIOCA

Wash and clean peas, beans, carrots, lima beans, green pepper, celery, onion, and parsley, and chop very fine. Place meat in a large kettle and add all other ingredients except tapioca. Cover with water and place over a low fire. Cook for 6 to 8 hours.

Remove fat from surface, add tapioca, and let simmer until ready to use. Add a little more water if it seems too thick. This burns easily, so keep the fire low. If it sticks to the pan, do not scrape off. Pour immediately into another pan. Serves 6 to 10.

S A N D W I C H E S

SANDWICH SUGGESTIONS

1. Chopped hard-boiled eggs, curry powder, mayonnaise, salt, and pepper.
2. Mashed liverwurst, mayonnaise, Worcestershire sauce, and freshly ground pepper.
3. Chopped chicken, chopped blanched almonds, and mayonnaise.
4. Grated American cheese, chopped onions, sardines, and lemon juice.
5. Cream cheese, horseradish, French dressing, chopped nuts, chopped celery, onion juice, Tabasco sauce, Worcestershire sauce, cayenne, and salt.
6. Minced ham, chopped hard-boiled eggs, chopped celery, onion juice, and mayonnaise.
7. Cream cheese, orange marmalade, and chopped pecans on brown bread.
8. Chopped crisp bacon, chopped hard-boiled egg, and mayonnaise.
9. Softened cream cheese spread on nut bread and topped with thin slices of strawberries.
10. Ground raisins, crumbled crisp bacon, lemon juice, and mayonnaise.
11. Smoked salmon on buttered, thinly sliced rye bread.

LUNCHEON SANDWICH

HAM
SWISS CHEESE
TURKEY
RYE BREAD

COLESLAW
THOUSAND ISLAND
DRESSING

Place a slice of ham, then a thin slice of Swiss cheese, then a slice of turkey on a buttered round of rye bread. Top with well-seasoned coleslaw and pour Thousand Island dressing over all.

GREEN AND WHITE SANDWICHES

2 3-OZ PKGS CREAM
   CHEESE
2 GREEN BELL PEPPERS
2 SMALL ONIONS
4 CELERY STALKS
   MAYONNAISE

SALT
PAPRIKA
TOAST ROUNDS
STUFFED OLIVES

Mash cream cheese. Clean vegetables and put them through a food grinder. Combine with cheese. Blend in mayonnaise until mixture is of spreading consistency. Add salt and paprika to taste. Spread on buttered rounds of bread and top each with a slice of stuffed olive.

CUCUMBER CHEESE SANDWICHES

1 3-OZ PKG CREAM
   CHEESE
1 SMALL CUCUMBER
   FRENCH DRESSING

ONION JUICE
SALT
CAYENNE PEPPER

Mash cream cheese. Blend in cucumber that has been peeled, grated, and drained well (should make about 2 tablespoons). Add the remaining ingredients to taste and mix well. Spread on buttered bread. Makes about 10 small tea sandwiches.

CHEESE DREAM

CHEESE	2 SLICES BREAD
CAYENNE PEPPER	BUTTER

S prinkle slice of cheese with cayenne pepper. Place between two thin slices of bread and sauté both sides in butter until browned.

CHEESE AND ANCHOVY PASTE

2 TBSP BUTTER	¼ TSP CAYENNE
¼ C AMERICAN CHEESE, GRATED	¼ TSP PAPRIKA
1 TSP ANCHOVY PASTE	¼ TSP DRY MUSTARD
1 TSP LEMON JUICE	1 TBSP CHOPPED AND STUFFED OLIVES
¼ TSP SALT	

C ream butter, blend in finely grated cheese, and add the remaining ingredients. Mix well and spread on whole-wheat bread.

ONION SANDWICHES

BERMUDA ONIONS	BUTTER
SUGAR	BOSTON BROWN
CREAM CHEESE	BREAD
MAYONNAISE	WHITE BREAD

C ut large Bermuda onions in thin slices and soak in iced, sweetened water until crisp. Drain and dry. Soften cream cheese with mayonnaise and season well. Spread thin buttered rounds of Boston brown bread and white bread with cheese mixture. Place an onion slice between contrasting rounds.

SOUTHERN HAM SALAD

4	C BAKED OR BOILED HAM, GROUND	1	MEDIUM GREEN BELL PEPPER
3	HARD-BOILED EGGS	¼	C SUGAR
12	SWEET PICKLES	½	C VINEGAR
1	2-OZ CAN PIMIENTO	1½	C MAYONNAISE

Trim all fat and gristle from ham. Put ham, eggs, pickles, pimiento, and green pepper through food grinder, using fine blade. Mix with sugar, vinegar, and mayonnaise. Serve with lettuce in sandwiches, on rounds of toast, on crackers with soup or salad, or as appetizers. Makes about 80 small canapés or 20 sandwiches.

CHEESE BUNS

1	LB SHARP CHEESE	½	TSP PAPRIKA
1	2-OZ CAN PIMIENTOS		SALT TO TASTE
1	TSP PREPARED MUSTARD		ONION JUICE
1	TSP WORCESTERSHIRE SAUCE		MAYONNAISE
½	TSP TABASCO SAUCE		FINGER ROLLS
			BACON STRIPS

Finely grate cheese. Mince pimiento. Add mustard, Worcestershire sauce, Tabasco sauce, paprika, and salt, and mix well. Blend in onion juice to taste and mayonnaise to moisten.

Split finger rolls down the center without cutting through the bottom. Fill each with some of the cheese mixture. Cut bacon strips in half or thirds and lay a piece on top of each roll lengthwise, securing with toothpicks. Place under a medium broiler flame and cook until bacon is crisp and cheese is melted.

This mixture will fill 3 dozen large finger rolls, or 5 to 6 dozen small.

SHRIMP RAREBIT SANDWICHES

1	TBSP MINCED ONION	1	PIMIENTO,
2	TBSP BUTTER		THINLY SLICED
1	C COOKED WHOLE		TOAST
	SHRIMP	1	8-OZ PKG SHARP
1	GREEN BELL PEPPER,		AMERICAN CHEESE
	SEEDED AND SLICED	¼	C MILK

Sauté onion in butter until tender but not brown. Add shrimp, green pepper, and pimiento. Heat well and place on hot toast slices.

Melt cheese with milk in the top of a double boiler. Stir until smooth and pour over shrimp. Serves 2 to 4.

S E A F O O D

BAKED FISH WITH CHEESE SAUCE

4	LBS FISH STEAKS	BUTTER
	(FLOUNDER,	SALT TO TASTE
	HALIBUT, ETC.)	JUICE OF 1 LEMON

Rub fish with butter; sprinkle with salt and lemon juice. Place in a greased pan and bake at 400°F for 30 minutes. Cover with the sauce.

CHEESE SAUCE

½	C BUTTER		SALT TO TASTE
4	TBSP FLOUR		DASH OF CAYENNE
2	C CREAM	2½	C CUBED SHARP
1	TSP MUSTARD		CHEESE

Melt butter. Add flour and stir until smooth. Mix in cream and seasonings. Cook over boiling water until mixture is the consistency of heavy cream. Add cheese and stir until melted. Pour over fish. Reduce oven temperature to 350°F and bake for 20 minutes more. Serves 8 to10.

GRILLED TROUT

6   BUTTERFLY FILLETED   BOTTLED ITALIAN
     TROUT (6–8 OZ EACH)   DRESSING
                                      BUTTER
                                      ALMONDS

Place trout in bowl or glass pan; cover with salad dressing. Marinate in refrigerator minimum of 4 hours. Place opened trout on grill, skin side down, over medium-hot coals. Grill until flesh turns white and flakes easily with a fork (about 10 to 15 minutes, depending on size of trout). Do not overcook. Do not turn. While grilling, melt butter; toast almonds in small skillet over very low heat. To serve, spoon butter over trout and sprinkle with toasted almonds. Serves 6.

SHRIMP NUECES

1   EGG, BEATEN WELL   MINCED FRESH
1   C SALAD OIL   PARSLEY
⅓   C CIDER VINEGAR   1   HARD-BOILED EGG,
¼   C PREPARED   CHOPPED
     MUSTARD   2   TSP CHOPPED CAPERS
1   GARLIC CLOVE,   SALT TO TASTE
     MINCED   2½–3   LBS COOKED SHRIMP
                                     PEPPER TO TASTE

Add oil very slowly to egg while beating, as in making mayonnaise. When thick, mix in remaining ingredients (vinegar through salt) one at a time, adding parsley to taste. Combine well.

Marinate shrimp in sauce for 4 to 6 hours before serving, then sprinkle with freshly ground black pepper. This recipe cannot be doubled. Serves 25.

SALMON-CORN SCALLOP

1	7½-OZ CAN PINK OR RED SALMON	1	C MILK
½	C CHOPPED ONIONS	1	16–17-OZ CAN CREAM-STYLE CORN
¼	C CHOPPED GREEN BELL PEPPER	2	EGGS, SLIGHTLY BEATEN
3	TBSP MARGARINE	1	C SHREDDED SHARP CHEDDAR CHEESE
1¼	C CRUSHED WATER CRACKERS	¼	TSP PEPPER

Drain and flake salmon. Set aside. Sauté onions and green pepper in 2 tablespoons margarine for 5 to 10 minutes, or until tender. Stir in flaked salmon, 1 cup cracker crumbs, milk, corn, eggs, cheese, and pepper. Turn into an 8 x 8 x 2-inch baking dish. Melt remaining margarine; toss with remaining cracker crumbs and sprinkle over casserole. Bake uncovered at 350°F for 30 minutes, or until knife inserted in center comes out clean. Serves 6.

TROUT MARGUERY

3–4	LBS TROUT	2	DOZ SHRIMP
6	TBSP OLIVE OIL	1	10½-OZ CAN MUSHROOMS, DRAINED
	SALT AND PEPPER TO TASTE		
1	C WATER	1	CAN TRUFFLES, JULIENNE
4	EGG YOLKS		
1	LB BUTTER, MELTED		
	JUICE OF 2 LEMONS		

Have trout skinned, boned, and cut into fillets. Roll in olive oil and place in a greased baking pan. Add salt, pepper, and water. Bake at 450°F for about 20 minutes or until done. Place on individual plates and keep hot.

Put egg yolks in the top of a double boiler. Add melted butter while beating constantly until thick. Add lemon juice, shrimp, mushrooms, and truffles. Mix in some of the drippings from the fish. Pour over trout and serve immediately. Serves 4.

CRAB CASSEROLE

¼	C BUTTER, MELTED	1	TBSP MAYONNAISE
1	TSP SALT	1	C HEAVY CREAM
1	TSP PEPPER	1	EGG, BEATEN
3	TBSP FLOUR	1	LB LUMP CRABMEAT
½	TSP WORCESTERSHIRE SAUCE	1	TBSP CHOPPED FRESH PARSLEY
½	TSP PREPARED MUSTARD		

Make a sauce with the butter, salt and pepper, flour, Worcestershire sauce, mustard, mayonnaise, and cream. Carefully add egg and mix with crab and parsley. Pour into buttered casserole from which it can be served. Bake 15 to 20 minutes at 375°F. Serves 4.

PAN-FRIED TROUT

4	TROUT (8–10 OZ EACH), COMPLETELY THAWED IF FROZEN	½	C FLOUR
		3	TBSP BUTTER
2	TSP SALT	6	TBSP VEGETABLE OIL
¼	TSP PEPPER	1	LEMON, CUT INTO WEDGES
½	C YELLOW CORNMEAL		

Wash trout briefly under cold, running water. Pat dry inside and out with paper towels. Sprinkle cavities and skins with salt and pepper. Mix cornmeal and flour. In heavy 12-inch skillet, melt the butter with the oil over moderate heat. When the foam begins to subside, roll each trout in the cornmeal-flour mixture, shake off excess, and place trout in the skillet. Fry 4 to 5 minutes on each side, until golden brown and crisp and flaky when probed with a fork. Serve with lemon wedges. Serves 4.

BOUILLABAISSE ORLEANS

8	LBS ASSORTED FISH, SLICED (SAVE HEADS AND TAILS FOR STOCK)	4	C DRY WHITE WINE
3	BAY LEAVES	3	SPRIGS THYME (OR PINCHES OF GROUND THYME)
1	C SPANISH OLIVE OIL	6	PINCHES ALLSPICE
6	HOT SPANISH ONIONS, FINELY CHOPPED		SALT, PEPPER, AND CAYENNE TO TASTE*
3	GARLIC CLOVES, FINELY CHOPPED	2	PINCHES SAFFRON
8	LARGE TOMATOES OR 2 20-OZ CANS OF TOMATOES	24	SLICES FRENCH BREAD FRIED IN BUTTER OR TOASTED TORTILLAS
		1	C CHOPPED PARSLEY LEMON

Boil fish heads, tails, and shells in 2 quarts of salted water to which you have added the bay leaves. Heat the olive oil in a large skillet, and when really hot, brown the slices of fish in it and then remove and drain them on paper towels. Brown the chopped onions and garlic, and add tomatoes, wine, thyme, allspice, salt, and peppers. Let the fish stock simmer until it has boiled down to only 1 quart, or half the original amount. Strain and add this to the skillet along with the browned slices of fish. Cover tightly and cook for 15 minutes while you mix the saffron with just enough wine to dissolve it. Arrange the slices of toast on a large platter. Pour the bouillabaisse over the toast after adding the saffron. Top with chopped parsley and garnish with thin slices of lemon.

*Chopped fresh hot chile peppers may be substituted for pepper.

BAKED AVOCADOS WITH TUNA

1	C THICK CREAM SAUCE	1	TSP GRATED GREEN BELL PEPPER
1	6-OZ CAN TUNA FEW DROPS WORCESTERSHIRE SAUCE		SALT AND PEPPER TO TASTE
2	TSP GRATED ONION	¼	C SHERRY
2	TSP PREPARED HORSERADISH	2	AVOCADOS LEMON JUICE GRATED CHEDDAR CHEESE

Drain oil/water from tuna and add to cream sauce (see "Sauces"). Add Worcestershire sauce, onion, horseradish, green pepper, and seasonings. Add sherry last.

Cut avocados in half, remove pits, and rub insides with lemon juice. Pile each with part of the creamed mixture. Cover with grated cheese. Place in a long pan of hot water (just covering the bottom of the pan), and bake at 350°F for 15 minutes. Serve immediately. Serves 4. (Shrimp, crabmeat, lobster, or chicken may be substituted for the tuna fish.)

BAKED FISH WITH CRABMEAT

6–8	LBS REDFISH OR RED SNAPPER	2	LBS CRABMEAT
1	GREEN BELL PEPPER	1	C BUTTER, MELTED
1	LARGE ONION		SALT AND PEPPER
		3	C CREOLE SAUCE

Split fish in half through the center and debone. Place half on a greased baking dish, cut side up. Mince green pepper and onion, clean crabmeat, combine with vegetables, and spread on fish. Pour butter over this. Place the second half of the fish on top of the stuffing, cut side down. Tie together with a heavy cord. Sprinkle with salt and pepper. Pour Creole sauce (see "Sauces") over all. Bake at 350°F for 45 minutes, basting occasionally. Serves 10.

Put any leftover fish in a dish and pour remaining sauce over it. Place in the refrigerator overnight and it will congeal like tomato aspic. Slice and serve with mayonnaise.

DEVILED CRABS

8	TBSP BUTTER	1	TSP WORCESTERSHIRE
4	TBSP FLOUR		SAUCE
1	C MILK		DASH OF TABASCO
2	6½-OZ CANS		SAUCE
	CRABMEAT	1	TBSP MINCED FRESH
1	TSP SALT		PARSLEY
	PEPPER TO TASTE		SMALL CRAB SHELLS
1	TSP PREPARED	½	C TOASTED CRACKER
	MUSTARD		CRUMBS
		2	EGGS, WELL BEATEN

Melt 4 tablespoons butter and blend in flour. Add milk and cook, stirring constantly, until very thick. Remove from fire and mix in clean crabmeat, salt, pepper, mustard, Worcestershire sauce, Tabasco sauce, and parsley. Stir in one-fourth cup of the cracker crumbs and the eggs. Place in crab shells. Top with the remaining crumbs and dot with remaining butter. Bake at 350°F for about 10 minutes, or until browned. This recipe fills 8 small shells.

JAMBALAYA LAFITTE

1	TBSP SHORTENING		MINCED FRESH
1	TBSP FLOUR		PARSLEY TO TASTE
1	SLICE HAM, DICED		MINCED GARLIC
	(OPTIONAL)		TO TASTE
2	CUPS COOKED	1	RED PEPPER POD
	CHICKEN, DICED		SALT AND PEPPER
1	LB LIGHTLY		TO TASTE
	SEASONED SAUSAGE	1	C LONG-GRAINED
1	LB SHRIMP, COOKED		RICE
	AND CLEANED	1½	C WATER
1	10-OZ CAN TOMATOES	18	OYSTERS
¾	CHOPPED ONION		
½	C CHOPPED GREEN		
	ONION TOPS		

Melt shortening in a heavy iron pot. Blend in flour and brown lightly. Add ham and brown. Mix in chicken, sausage, shrimp, and tomatoes. Cover and cook for 20 minutes.

Stir in remaining ingredients except oysters. Cook, covered, for about 20 minutes, or until rice is tender. Add oysters and simmer until their edges curl. Serves 8 to 12.

SPAGHETTI WITH OYSTERS

6	TBSP OLIVE OIL	2	TBSP SALT
2–4	GARLIC CLOVES, VERY FINELY CHOPPED	½	LB SPAGHETTINI OR SPAGHETTI
12	FRESH OYSTERS AND JUICE		PEPPER
			CHOPPED FRESH
6	TBSP BUTTER		PARSLEY
1½	GALLONS BOILING WATER		GRATED PARMESAN CHEESE

Sauté garlic in olive oil over a low flame until golden brown. Add oysters and juice. Continue to simmer until oysters curl. Mix in butter and remove from the fire.

Cook spaghetti in salted water for about 9 minutes, or until tender, stirring frequently. Place in a colander, rinse with additional boiling water, and drain well. Add spaghetti to oyster sauce and cook over a low flame, stirring constantly, until very hot. Serve sprinkled heavily with pepper, parsley, and Parmesan cheese. Serves 2 to 4.

TOMATOES STUFFED WITH SHRIMP

6	MEDIUM TOMATOES	¼	TSP THYME
1	MEDIUM ONION	2	BAY LEAVES
6	TBSP BUTTER		SALT AND PEPPER
4	SLICES DRY BREAD	2	5-OZ CANS SHRIMP
2	TBSP MINCED PARSLEY		

Hollow out unpeeled tomatoes, turn upside down and drain. Chop insides fine and reserve. Peel and mince onion and sauté slowly in 1 tablespoon of the butter until tender and golden.

Soak bread in a little water. Squeeze dry. Season with parsley, thyme, crushed bay leaves, and salt and pepper to taste. Sauté this in 2 tablespoons butter until the water is cooked out.

Combine chopped tomatoes, onion, bread mixture, and drained chopped shrimp. Mix well and stuff tomato shells. Top each with a small piece of remaining butter. Place in a greased pan and bake at 325°F for 20 minutes, or until tomatoes are tender. Serves 6.

SALMON PUDDING

2	LBS RAW SALMON		SALT AND PEPPER
1	C CREAM SAUCE		DRY MUSTARD
2	TBSP BUTTER		HEAVY CREAM
4	MUSHROOMS		BREADCRUMBS
3	EGG YOLKS		GRATED CHEESE
3	EGG WHITES, STIFFLY BEATEN	3	TBSP FLOUR

Skin and bone salmon, put it through a meat grinder, and add cream sauce. Mix in mushrooms (sliced and sautéed in butter), egg yolks, and whites. Season and add cream. Put in well-greased baking dish and top with breadcrumbs and cheese. Place in a pan of hot water and bake 35 minutes at 350°F.

CREAM SAUCE

2	TBSP BUTTER	2	TBSP GRATED PARMESAN CHEESE
2	TBSP FLOUR		
1	C MILK	¼	C HEAVY CREAM, WHIPPED
1	EGG YOLK		

In heavy pan, melt butter, blend in flour and slowly stir in milk, cooking until thickened. When thickened, add egg yolk, grated Parmesan cheese, and whipped cream.

OYSTER STEW

1	TBSP BUTTER		DASH OF CELERY SALT
½	C OYSTER LIQUOR		DASH OF SWEET
3	DROPS		PAPRIKA
	WORCESTERSHIRE	1⅓	C LIGHT CREAM
	SAUCE	8	OYSTERS
	DASH OF SALT		CAYENNE PEPPER
	DASH OF PEPPER		

Melt butter in the top of a double boiler, with water underneath kept just at the boiling point. Mix in oyster liquor, Worcestershire sauce, and seasonings (except cayenne). Cook for 2 minutes. Stir in cream and continue to cook only long enough to heat. Pour over oysters that have been placed in a warm soup plate. Top with 1 teaspoon butter and a dash of cayenne pepper. Serves 1.

SCALLOPED OYSTERS

1	QT SMALL OYSTERS	1	C LIGHT CREAM
	SALT AND PEPPER	2	TBSP SHERRY
24	SODA CRACKERS		PAPRIKA
½	C BUTTER		

Drain oysters. Place half of them in the bottom of a greased 8-inch casserole. Sprinkle with salt and pepper. Crush crackers into fine crumbs and put a layer of them over the oysters. Mix cream and sherry. Dot with half the butter, pour in half the cream and sherry mixture and then repeat. Sprinkle with paprika. Bake at 400°F for about 45 minutes, or until brown. Serves 6.

HALIBUT-CITRUS AMANDINE

⅓ C SLIVERED ALMONDS
1 TBSP OLIVE OIL
⅓ C THINLY SLICED
GREEN ONIONS
1 TSP MINCED GARLIC
1 TSP GRATED RUBY-
RED OR PINK
GRAPEFRUIT PEEL

4 PORTIONS (ABOUT 6
OZ EACH) SKINLESS
HALIBUT FILETS
3 RED OR PINK
GRAPEFRUIT
SALT AND PEPPER
TO TASTE

Heat oven to 425°F. In medium nonstick skillet over medium heat, toss almonds in oil about 2 minutes until lightly browned. Remove from heat; mix in onions, garlic, and peel. Arrange fish in shallow baking pan. Juice one of the grapefruit; pour juice over fish, then top evenly with almond mixture. Bake in center of oven 10 to 12 minutes until fish flakes when tested with a fork and is opaque throughout. (Baking time will depend on thickness of fish). Meanwhile, peel and section remaining grapefruit. Season fish with salt and pepper and arrange on platter. Pour over any pan juices and surround with grapefruit sections. Serves 4.

PAN-FRIED WALLEYE

2–2½ LBS FRESH WALLEYE
FILLETS OR OTHER
SIMILAR FISH
SALT AND PEPPER
TO TASTE
4 TBSP FLOUR,
SEASONED WITH SALT
AND PEPPER

1 SMALL EGG
¼ C MILK
1 C WHITE
BREADCRUMBS
⅜ C SOYBEAN, PEANUT,
OR CANOLA OIL

Check fish for bones, remove skin, and cut into four portions. Season fish; dredge in flour. Beat egg and milk. Dip fish in egg mixture and drain; dust with breadcrumbs. Heat a large skillet, add oil, and panfry on low heat. Serve immediately. Serves 4.

FILLETS OF FLOUNDER

4 FILLETS OF
FLOUNDER OR
OTHER FISH
FLOUR, SEASONED
WITH SALT AND
PEPPER
1 5-OZ CAN SHRIMP,
DRAINED

½ C SHERRY
½ C HEAVY CREAM
GRATED PARMESAN
CHEESE
WHITE SEEDLESS
GRAPES

Dip fillets in seasoned flour. Place in a greased casserole. Add shrimp and sherry. Bake at 350°F for 10 minutes. Pour in cream and sprinkle with cheese. Continue to cook for 10 minutes more. Just before serving, dot with grapes. Serves 4.

SHRIMP ARNAUD

4 TBSP OLIVE OIL
2 TBSP LEMON JUICE
4 TBSP VINEGAR
2 TBSP DRY MUSTARD
½ TSP PAPRIKA
2 GARLIC CLOVES,
FINELY CHOPPED

2 CELERY STALKS,
FINELY CHOPPED
1 TBSP FINELY
CHOPPED FRESH
PARSLEY
SALT AND PEPPER
TO TASTE
1 LB SHRIMP, COOKED
AND CLEANED

Blend all ingredients together, except shrimp. Chill. Mix with chilled shrimp. Serve on lettuce or in cocktail glasses. Serves 4.

LUNCHEON SHRIMP

2 LBS SHRIMP	JUICE OF 2 LEMONS
1 C CHOPPED CELERY	1 TSP WORCESTERSHIRE
1 C CHOPPED GREEN	SAUCE
BELL PEPPER	3 C CREAM SAUCE
1 C CHOPPED ONION	1 C GRATED SHARP
1½ C WATER	CHEESE
1 C KETCHUP	1 C BUTTERED
1 C COOKED PEAS	CRACKER CRUMBS

Cook and clean shrimp. Boil celery, green pepper, and onion in water until mushy. Drain and add to shrimp. Combine with ketchup, peas, lemon juice, and Worcestershire sauce.

Add cheese to hot cream sauce (see "Sauces") and stir until melted. Place a layer of shrimp mixture in the bottom of a greased casserole and cover with a layer of cream sauce. Repeat until all ingredients are used, reserving 1 cup of the cream sauce for the top. Cover with cracker crumbs. Bake at 350°F for 45 minutes. Serve with or on rice. Serves 8 to 10.

SHRIMP REMOULADE

2 3-OZ PKG CREAM	½ C MAYONNAISE
CHEESE	SALT AND PAPRIKA
¼ C OLIVE OIL	TO TASTE
¼ C GARLIC RED WINE	MINCED ONION AND
VINEGAR	GARLIC TO TASTE
4 TBSP HORSERADISH	1 LB LARGE SHRIMP,
MUSTARD	COOKED

Mix cream cheese, olive oil, vinegar, mayonnaise, mustard, salt, paprika, onion, and garlic until smooth. Add shrimp and let stand in the refrigerator for at least 1 hour before serving. The shrimp and sauce may also be served separately, without marinating ahead of time. Serves 4.

REDFISH PIQUANT

1	LARGE ONION	1	TBSP KETCHUP
1	LARGE GREEN BELL PEPPER	1	TSP CHILI POWDER DASH OF TABASCO
2	C CHOPPED CELERY	2	BAY LEAVES
2	TBSP BUTTER	1	GARLIC CLOVE
1	19-OZ CAN TOMATOES	½	LEMON, THINLY SLICED
1	TBSP WORCESTERSHIRE SAUCE	3	LBS REDFISH FLOUR
2½	TSP SALT		

Clean and chop onion and green pepper. Combine with celery and sauté in butter for 15 minutes. Mix in tomatoes, Worcestershire sauce, salt, ketchup, chili powder, Tabasco, bay leaves, garlic, and lemon. Cover and cook slowly for about 30 minutes, or until celery is tender. Press through a sieve.

Clean and bone fish, leaving it whole. Rub inside and out with salt and pepper, and dredge with flour. Place in a greased baking dish and pour sauce over and around it. Bake at 450°F for 1 hour, basting frequently. Serves 4.

FISH AND CHEESE CASSEROLE

2	TBSP MINCED ONION	1	7-OZ CAN FLAKED FISH
1	TBSP MINCED GREEN BELL PEPPER	2	HARD-BOILED EGGS, CHOPPED
3	TBSP BUTTER	½	C SOFT BREADCRUMBS
1	C MEDIUM WHITE SAUCE	½	C GRATED AMERICAN CHEESE
1	TBSP A-1 SAUCE		

Sauté onion and green pepper in butter until tender. Add to white sauce (see "Sauces"). Mix in A-1, fish, and eggs. Place in a greased casserole and top with crumbs that have been combined with cheese. Bake at 350°F for 20 to 30 minutes, or until well heated and crumbs are brown.

This may be prepared the day before and then reheated. Cooked or canned flaked tuna, salmon, crabmeat, or lobster may be used. Serves 4.

CRAB AND SHRIMP ESPAÑOL

3	TBSP BUTTER	1	C CRABMEAT
1	TBSP MINCED GREEN	1	C COOKED SHRIMP
	BELL PEPPER	1	C COOKED
1	TSP MINCED ONION		MUSHROOMS
1	TBSP FLOUR	¼	TSP SALT
¾	C MILK		DASH OF PEPPER
1	TSP CHILI POWDER		CAYENNE
1	TBSP CHILI SAUCE OR		
	KETCHUP		

Sauté green pepper and onion in 2 tablespoons of the butter until browned. Remove from pan. Melt the remaining 1 tablespoon butter and blend in flour. Add milk, and cook, stirring constantly, until thickened. Mix in chili powder and pepper-onion mixture. Stir in the remaining ingredients and heat well. Serve over rice. Serves 6.

CRABMEAT AU GRATIN

2	6½-OZ CANS OF	1	7½-OZ CAN SLICED
	CRABMEAT		MUSHROOMS
1¾	C MEDIUM CREAM	1½	C AMERICAN CHEESE,
	SAUCE		GRATED
8	HARD-BOILED EGGS,		DASH OF PAPRIKA
	DICED		

Flake crabmeat and remove any pieces of shell. Combine all ingredients, stir in cream sauce (see "Sauces"), and mix well. Place in a greased casserole and bake at 350°F for 20 to 30 minutes, or until heated through and brown on top. Serves 10 to 12.

SHRIMP CREOLE

3	GREEN BELL PEPPERS, FINELY DICED		2	STICKS BUTTER OR ½ LB DICED RAW BACON
4	ONIONS, FINELY CHOPPED		3	46-OZ CANS TOMATOES
2	GARLIC CLOVES, FINELY CHOPPED		½	TSP BLACK PEPPER
4	C FINELY CHOPPED CELERY		1	TSP SALT
½	C MINCED FRESH PARSLEY		1	TSP CURRY POWDER
			1	TSP DRIED THYME
			½	TSP CAYENNE PEPPER
			5	LBS CLEANED RAW SHRIMP

Sauté peppers, onions, garlic, celery, and parsley in butter or bacon. Add tomatoes and seasonings and cook on low 30 minutes. Add raw shrimp and cook 20 minutes more. Serve with rice. Serves 8 to 10.

FRIED SHRIMP DELICIOUS

1	LB MEDIUM SHRIMP	FLOUR (FOR DREDGING)
1	EGG, WELL BEATEN	BREADCRUMBS OR
1	TSP SALT	CRACKER CRUMBS
1	TSP PAPRIKA	(FOR DREDGING)
	DASH OF CELERY SALT	VEGETABLE OIL
1	TSP PREPARED MUSTARD	(FOR DEEP-FRYING)
1	TBSP LEMON JUICE	PARSLEY OR
3	TBSP WATER	WATERCRESS

Shell and devein shrimp. Combine egg, salt, paprika, celery salt, mustard, lemon juice, and water. Roll shrimp in flour, then in egg mixture, and last in breadcrumbs. Fry until golden brown in oil heated to 370°F or hot enough to brown a 1-inch cube of bread in 60 seconds. Drain and serve at once, garnished with parsley or watercress. Serves 2.

SHRIMP GUMBO WITH RICE

STEP 1

1	QT BOILING WATER		DASH OF VINEGAR
1½	TSP SALT	1	TSP WORCESTERSHIRE
3	CLOVES		SAUCE
3	PEPPERCORNS	1	LB RAW SHRIMP,
	DASH OF TABASCO		PEELED AND
	RIND AND JUICE		CLEANED
	OF ½ LEMON		

Add all ingredients to boiling water in the order given. Cook slowly until shrimp are tender, 10 to 12 minutes for small ones, 15 to 20 for large. Cool. Drain shrimp, reserving liquor.

STEP 2

1	SMALL GREEN BELL		SHRIMP LIQUOR
	PEPPER, CHOPPED	1	29-OZ CAN TOMATOES
2	MEDIUM ONIONS,	1	20-OZ CAN OKRA,
	CHOPPED		DRAINED
1	GARLIC CLOVE,	2	TBSP GUMBO FILÉ
	MINCED	1	TSP SALT
3	TBSP BUTTER	¼	TSP PEPPER
1½	TBSP FLOUR		

Sauté green pepper, onion, and garlic in butter. Remove from pan and smooth in flour. Add shrimp liquor and stir well. Mix in tomatoes, then add green pepper, onion, and garlic mixture. Simmer for 1 hour. Mix in okra and cook 15 minutes more. Add shrimp and heat until warmed through. Just before serving add filé, salt, and pepper. Serve with rice. Serves 8.

FISH SOUFFLÉ

2	C WHITE SAUCE	2	EGG YOLKS, WELL
2	TSP CHOPPED		BEATEN
	PARSLEY	2	EGG WHITES, STIFFLY
1	TSP LEMON JUICE		BEATEN
2	TSP WORCESTERSHIRE	⅔	C GRATED AMERICAN
	SAUCE		OR CHEDDAR CHEESE
2	C COOKED FLAKED		
	FISH		

Add parsley, lemon juice, Worcestershire sauce, and fish to white sauce (see "Sauces"). Mix in egg yolks. Fold in egg whites. Pour into a greased casserole and top with cheese. Bake at 375°F for about 40 minutes, or until firm. Serves 6 to 8.

Lobster, crabmeat, shrimp, or tuna fish may be substituted for the flaked fish.

CRAWFISH ÉTOUFFÉE

¼	LB BUTTER OR	¼	C CHOPPED GREEN
	MARGARINE		ONION TOPS
1	C CHOPPED ONION	¼	C CHOPPED FRESH
1	C CHOPPED CELERY		PARSLEY
1	C CHOPPED BELL	1	8-OZ CAN TOMATO
	PEPPER		SAUCE, OPTIONAL
2	GARLIC CLOVES,	2	TSP CORNSTARCH
	MINCED	½	TSP PEPPER
1	C WATER	¼	TSP CAYENNE PEPPER
1	LB CRAWFISH TAILS		PAPRIKA FOR COLOR

Sauté onion, celery, bell pepper, and garlic in butter until tender crisp (about 5 minutes). Then add ½ cup water and simmer covered for 15 minutes, or until vegetables are tender. Stir in crawfish, green onion tops, parsley, and tomato sauce if used. Dissolve cornstarch in ½ cup water and add to mixture. Season to taste and mix thoroughly. Cover and cook 15 minutes, stirring occasionally. Serve hot over rice. Serves 5 to 6.

OYSTERS IN SHERRY CREAM

2	DOZ LARGE OYSTERS	¾	C CRACKER CRUMBS
	SALT AND PEPPER	2	TBSP SHERRY
	TO TASTE	1	C LIGHT CREAM

D rain oysters. Place them in a greased shallow pan and sprinkle with salt and pepper. Cover with cracker crumbs. Pour sherry, then cream, over this. Cook under broiler flame for two minutes. Turn and cook until edges are curled and the crumbs are browned. Serves 4.

BAKED SCALLOPS

2	HEAPING C SEA SCALLOPS	2	C DRY SHERRY
4	SHALLOTS, FINELY CHOPPED	2	TBSP SOFT BUTTER BLENDED WITH 2 TBSP FLOUR
4	TBSP BUTTER SALT TO TASTE	⅓	C BUTTERED CRACKER CRUMBS

S auté chopped shallots in butter in ovenproof pan. Add scallops, salt, and sherry. Cover and place in oven for 15 minutes at 350°F. Reduce sherry to one half. Remove scallops and thicken juices with flour and butter mixture, adding a little at a time. If necessary to moisten, add a little heated cream. Put scallops into serving casserole dish. Cover with sauce, add chopped chives and cracker crumbs, and bake in 425°F oven until golden brown. Watch closely.

RICE, EGG, CHEESE, AND PASTA DISHES

RUSSIAN RAREBIT

2	TBSP CHOPPED GREEN BELL PEPPER	1	TSP DRY MUSTARD
2	TBSP CHOPPED ONION	1	TSP WORCESTERSHIRE SAUCE
1½	TBSP BUTTER		CAYENNE PEPPER
1	LB AMERICAN CHEESE, GRATED		PAPRIKA
1	20-OZ CAN TOMATOES	1	EGG, WELL BEATEN
½	TSP SALT	2	TBSP FLOUR
		½	C HEAVY CREAM

Cook green pepper and onion in butter in the top of a double boiler for 20 to 30 minutes, or until very soft. Add cheese, tomatoes, salt, and mustard. When cheese begins to melt, mix in Worcestershire sauce, cayenne, and paprika to taste. Cook for 5 to 10 minutes.

Add flour and cream to egg and beat until smooth. Stir into cheese mixture 5 minutes before serving. Pour over toasted bread or crackers. Serves 4 to 6.

CHEESE SOUFFLÉ

1	C THICK WHITE SAUCE	3	EGG YOLKS, WELL BEATEN
1	C GRATED AMERICAN CHEESE	3	EGG WHITES, STIFFLY BEATEN

Add cheese to hot white sauce (see "Sauces"). Stir over a low flame until melted. Cool. Add egg yolks. Fold in egg whites. Pour into a greased casserole and set in a pan of warm water. Bake at 325°F for 50 to 60 minutes, or until firm. Serves 6.

POACHED EGGS GLAZED WITH HOLLANDAISE

6	EGGS	SALT AND PEPPER
2	TBSP SALT	TO TASTE
2	TBSP WHITE VINEGAR	DILL TO TASTE
3	TOMATOES	

Put water in skillet, add vinegar and salt. Bring to boil. Reduce heat and poach eggs in hot water. Leave them soft. Remove eggs from water with slotted spoon and drain on absorbent paper. Cut tomatoes in half, season with salt, pepper, and dill, and broil a few minutes. Put an egg on top of each tomato half and glaze with Hollandaise sauce (see "Sauces"). Serves 6.

BROWN RICE ROYALE

2   C (ABOUT 8 OZ) MUSHROOMS, SLICED
½   C THINLY SLICED GREEN ONIONS
1   TBSP VEGETABLE OIL
3   C COOKED BROWN RICE (COOKED IN CHICKEN OR VEGETABLE STOCK)

Cook mushrooms and onions in oil in large skillet over medium-high heat until tender. Add rice. Stir until thoroughly heated. Serves 6.

To microwave: Combine mushrooms, onions, and oil in 2-quart microwave-safe baking dish. Cook on high 2 to 3 minutes. Add rice; continue to cook on high 3 to 4 minutes, stirring after 2 minutes, or until thoroughly heated.

BARBECUE RICE

2   TBSP VEGETABLE OIL
1   C CHOPPED ONION
8   C COOKED RICE
1½   C BARBECUE SAUCE
½   C SLICED GREEN ONION TOPS
2   TSP GARLIC POWDER
2   TSP CHOPPED CILANTRO
1   TSP LIQUID SMOKE

Sauté onion in oil until transparent. Add next 6 ingredients; heat thoroughly. Serve with barbecue chicken breast. Serves 12.

SPINACH QUICHE

PASTRY

1½	C FLOUR	2	TBSP VEGETABLE
¼	TSP SALT		SHORTENING
¼	TSP SUGAR	6	TBSP BUTTER
		3	TBSP COLD WATER

Place flour, salt, and sugar in a bowl. Rub in the shortening and butter gently with fingertips until mixture resembles oatmeal. Stir in the water a little at a time, until dough holds together. Chill at least 1 to 2 hours. Preheat oven to 400°F. Roll out dough and line an 8- or 9-inch pan that is 1½ inches deep and has a removable bottom or use a scalloped tart pan. Do not stretch pastry. Flute edge of pastry shell with fingers. Prick bottom with fork, line with aluminum foil, parchment, or oiled brown paper and fill with dried beans to prevent pastry from shrinking. Bake 8 minutes or until pastry has set. Remove beans and paper and prick with fork again. Bake 2 or 3 minutes longer.

FILLING

2	TBSP BUTTER	2	TSP SALT
2	TBSP FINELY MINCED	¼	TSP NUTMEG
	SHALLOTS	1¼	C HEAVY CREAM,
2	C CHOPPED FRESH		SCALDED
	SPINACH	¼	C GRATED SWISS
⅛	TSP PEPPER		CHEESE
4	EGGS		

Preheat oven to 375°F. Melt butter, sauté shallots until tender. Add spinach; cover and simmer 5 minutes. Blend spinach mixture, seasonings, and eggs in blender for 20 seconds. Continue to blend, pouring in cream. Pour into pastry shell. Sprinkle with cheese. Bake 25 to 35 minutes until quiche is puffed and brown. Serves 6.

SPANISH RICE

2	TBSP BACON FAT	1	C UNCOOKED RICE
2	ONIONS, FINELY SLICED	1½	C TOMATO JUICE
2	BAY LEAVES	1	C BOILING WATER OR STOCK, IF NECESSARY
1	TSP DRIED SWEET BASIL		SALT AND PEPPER TO TASTE
½	C MINCED GREEN BELL PEPPER		

Sauté onions in bacon fat until soft. Add bay leaves, sweet basil, and green pepper. Add rice, tomato juice and bring to a boil. Add stock or water if rice becomes too dry. Stir well, cover, and bake at 375°F until rice is tender, about 35 to 45 minutes. Serves 4.

NO-CRUST QUICHE

2	SMALL ZUCCHINI, SLICED	3	C GRATED SWISS CHEESE
1	SMALL ONION, THINLY SLICED	1	TSP DRIED OREGANO
8	EGGS	1	TSP DRIED BASIL
			SALT AND PEPPER TO TASTE

Steam zucchini and onion until tender. Beat eggs and fold in grated cheese. When vegetables are soft, mash them and add to cheese and egg mixture, stirring to blend. Sprinkle oregano and basil. Add salt and pepper to taste. Put into heavy baking dish and bake at 325°F for 40 minutes. Serves 6.

HUEVOS RANCHEROS

6   TORTILLAS
    OIL FOR FRYING
    (ENOUGH TO COAT
    BOTTOM OF
    FRYING PAN)
1   ONION, CHOPPED
1   GARLIC CLOVE,
    MINCED

2   SMALL GREEN,
    PIQUANT CHILE
    PEPPERS, CHOPPED,
    OR 2 TBSP CHOPPED
    SWEET BELL PEPPER,
    WITH 2 DROPS OF
    TABASCO SAUCE
2   CUPS TOMATO SAUCE
6   EGGS

Fry the tortillas quickly, but do not allow them to become hard or crisp. Sauté the onion, garlic, and peppers and add tomato sauce. Cook for 5 minutes. Fry eggs sunny-side up, place each one on a tortilla, pour the tomato mixture over the top, and serve immediately. Sliced avocado and cheese goes very well with this dish. Serves 6.

FARMHOUSE EGGS

1½   C STALE
     BREADCRUMBS
1½   C GRATED CHEDDAR
     OR CHESHIRE CHEESE
6   EGGS

1½   C LIGHT CREAM
     SALT AND PEPPER
     TO TASTE

Cover bottom of a casserole with stale breadcrumbs, then cover the crumbs with a layer of grated cheese. Break 6 eggs into the dish, cover with another layer of breadcrumbs and cheese. Carefully pour in cream. Sprinkle with a thick layer of breadcrumbs and cheese. Season each layer with salt and pepper. Place in slow 325°F oven, and cook until eggs are set and crumbs and cheese are browned. Serves 4.

GOLDEN CHEESE AND HAM BAKE

5	SLICES SOFT BREAD, CUT INTO ½-INCH CUBES	2	C MILK
		½	TSP SALT
¾	LB GRATED LONGHORN CHEESE (ABOUT 3 C)		DASH OF CAYENNE PEPPER
			DASH OF MSG (OPTIONAL)
6	EGGS, SLIGHTLY BEATEN	½	C CHOPPED HAM
		¼	C GRATED ONION
½	TSP DRY MUSTARD		

Spread bread slices in a greased 2-quart dish. Sprinkle with grated cheese. Combine other ingredients and pour over cheese/bread mixture. Cover with foil and refrigerate 8 hours. Uncover and bake at 350°F for 45 minutes. Serves 6.

EGGS CREOLE

1	ONION		SALT
1	CELERY STALK		CHILI POWDER
1	GREEN BELL PEPPER		PEPPER
1	C MUSHROOMS	8	HARD-BOILED EGGS
2	TBSP BUTTER		BUTTERED BREADCRUMBS
2	C TOMATO JUICE		

Chop up celery, onion, green pepper, and mushrooms. Melt butter and add vegetables, along with the tomato juice, and bring to a boil. Add seasonings. Slice eggs and fill greased baking dish with alternate layers of eggs and sauce. Cover with buttered breadcrumbs. Bake at 300°F until thoroughly heated.

BAKED PASTA WITH FOUR CHEESES

1	LB ZITI, MOSTACCIOLI, OR OTHER MEDIUM PASTA SHAPE (UNCOOKED)	¾	C CHOPPED FRESH PARSLEY
1	32-OZ JAR OF YOUR FAVORITE PASTA SAUCE	4	OZ GRATED PARMESAN CHEESE
1	C LOW-FAT COTTAGE CHEESE	4	OZ GRATED MOZZARELLA CHEESE
		4	OZ PROVOLONE CHEESE, CUT IN QUARTERS

Cook pasta according to package directions; drain. Coat 13 x 9 x 2 inch baking dish with cooking spray; set aside. Place a thin layer of sauce in bottom of prepared dish. Continue making layers of pasta, cottage cheese, parsley, sauce, pasta, Parmesan, pasta, Mozzarella, parsley, pasta, sauce, and parsley. Sprinkle Provolone on top. Cover and bake at 375°F for about 30 minutes or until cheese melts. Serves 8.

P O U L T R Y
A N D   G A M E

NEW BARBECUE CHICKEN

3 LBS CHICKEN PARTS
(BREAST, LEG, THIGH),
SKIN, FAT REMOVED
1 LARGE ONION,
THINLY SLICED
3 TBSP VINEGAR
3 TBSP
WORCESTERSHIRE
SAUCE

2 TBSP BROWN SUGAR
DASH OF PEPPER
1 TBSP HOT PEPPER
FLAKES
1 TBSP CHILI POWDER
1 C CHICKEN STOCK,
FAT REMOVED

Place chicken in a 13 x 9 x 2 pan. Arrange onions over the top. Mix together vinegar, Worcestershire sauce, brown sugar, pepper, hot pepper flakes, chili powder, and stock. Pour over the chicken and bake at 350°F for 1 hour or until done. Baste occasionally. Serves 8. Serve with cornbread and a salad made with distinctive greens.

BARBECUED CHICKEN IN CABBAGE

1	FRYER	½	C CHOPPED ONION
	CABBAGE	½	C BARBECUE SAUCE
	GARLIC		BACON
	SALT AND PEPPER		

Rub 1 small tender young fryer with garlic, salt, and pepper. Arrange 3 large coarse cabbage leaves, one overlapping the other, and place whole chicken in this nest. Put ¼ cup chopped onion and ¼ cup barbecue sauce in cavity. Brush skin with remaining barbecue sauce and cover with remaining chopped onion. Cross breast with 2 strips of bacon. Wrap in two layers of cabbage leaves and tie with strong white string. Allow 2 persons per chicken. Place over low fire in pit and cook for at least 6 to 7 hours. Baste the balls of cabbage frequently with the following sauce, keeping leaves pretty wet, and turn the balls over every half hour or so.

BASTING SAUCE

4	C WATER	2	TSP WORCESTERSHIRE
2	C VINEGAR		SAUCE
1	C BACON GREASE	1	TSP DRY MUSTARD
1	TBSP CHILI POWDER		SALT, PEPPER,
			CAYENNE

This thin, economical sauce is recommended since it should be used lavishly in the cooking process.

ENGLISH BOILED CHICKEN WITH PARSLEY SAUCE

1	4-LB CHICKEN	1	C MILK
2	ONIONS	1	C CHICKEN STOCK
1	CARROT		SALT AND PEPPER
2	CELERY STALKS	2	TBSP MINCED
2	BAY LEAVES		FRESH PARSLEY
2	TBSP BUTTER		JUICE OF 1 LEMON
2	TBSP FLOUR		

Boil the chicken with onion, carrots, celery, and bay leaves until tender. When done, remove from stock and keep warm on a separate platter. Make a sauce of butter, flour, milk, chicken stock, salt and pepper, minced parsley, and lemon juice. Slice the chicken, place on hot serving plate, and coat with the parsley sauce. Serves 6.

Both chicken and sauce may be prepared the day before serving, omitting parsley and lemon juice until ready to serve.

DOVE OR QUAIL

4	DOVES OR QUAIL		JUICE OF 1 LEMON
	SALT AND PEPPER	½	C WATER
	BACON DRIPPINGS		

Clean birds and split them down the back. Sprinkle with salt and pepper. Brown in bacon drippings in a heavy skillet for 20 minutes, turning frequently.

Add lemon juice and water. Cover and bake at 350°F for about 45 minutes or until tender. Baste frequently during baking, adding water if necessary to prevent sticking. Serves 2.

PAELLA

1	3-LB FRYING CHICKEN OLIVE OIL	4	TOMATOES, PEELED AND CHOPPED
2	GREEN BELL PEPPERS, CHOPPED	2	C UNCOOKED RICE
4	ONIONS, PEELED AND CHOPPED	2	LBS COOKED SHRIMP
4	GARLIC CLOVES, CHOPPED	10	GRAINS SAFFRON
		4	C CHICKEN STOCK SALT AND PEPPER

Cut chicken into serving pieces. Sauté in olive oil in a heavy iron skillet until brown and partially cooked. Add green pepper, onion, and garlic. Cook for 2 minutes. Mix in tomatoes. Cook 1 minute more. Stir in the remaining ingredients, using salt and pepper to taste.

Cover and cook on top of the stove over a low flame for 30 to 40 minutes, or until well heated. Pour into a greased 2-quart casserole, cover, and bake at 400°F for 30 to 40 minutes, until rice is tender. Garnish with parsley and cooked green peas. Serve with chilled dry sauterne. Serves 8.

HAWAIIAN CHICKEN ADOBO (STEW)

3	LBS CHICKEN THIGHS, CUT INTO SERVING PIECES	1	TSP BROWN SUGAR
½	C WHITE VINEGAR	5	GARLIC CLOVES, CRUSHED
½	C SOY SAUCE	3	BAY LEAVES SALT TO TASTE
¼	C PEPPERCORNS, CRUSHED		

Combine all ingredients in a pan, cover, and allow to marinate 1 to 3 hours. Bring to a boil, then lower heat and simmer for 30 minutes. Uncover pan and allow to simmer for an additional 15 minutes or until most of the liquid has evaporated and chicken is slightly brown. Remove bay leaves. Serve with white rice. Serves 4 to 6.

STUFFED BROILED CHICKEN

4	1½-LB BROILER CHICKENS	2	EGGS, BEATEN
½	LB MUSHROOMS, CHOPPED		SALT AND PEPPER TO TASTE
1	LARGE ONION, CHOPPED		POULTRY SEASONING TO TASTE
½	C BUTTER		MELTED BUTTER (FOR BASTING)
2	C COOKED RICE		JUICE OF 1 ORANGE

Split four 1½-lb chickens almost through and place skin side down on buttered ovenproof dish and broil for 15 minutes. Sauté mushrooms and onion in butter until tender. Add rice and mix well with eggs, salt, pepper, and poultry seasoning. Stuff into chickens. Turn skin side up and broil slowly for 30 minutes, basting generously with melted butter to which orange juice has been added. Cook until thoroughly done. Serve with watercress and pickled pears. Serves 8.

GRILLED CHICKEN WITH PEACH TERIYAKI BARBECUE SAUCE

20	BONELESS, SKINLESS CHICKEN BREAST HALVES

PEACH TERIYAKI BARBECUE SAUCE

20	FRESH PEACHES	10	TSP GRATED FRESH GINGER
10	TBSP BOTTLED LOW-SODIUM TERIYAKI MARINADE AND SAUCE	5	TSP DARK SESAME OIL
		1¼	TSP HOT PEPPER SAUCE

Finely dice peaches and mix well with 6 tablespoons plus 2 teaspoons of the teriyaki sauce, ginger, sesame oil, and hot sauce. Rub both sides of chicken with the remaining 2 tablespoons plus 1 teaspoon of the teriyaki sauce. Grill over medium coals for 15 minutes or until done but still juicy. Drizzle peach teriyaki sauce over chicken to serve.

SPANISH CHICKEN STEW

1	4-LB CHICKEN, CUT UP	1	TSP SALT
3	TBSP SHORTENING OR SALAD OIL	½	TSP GRANULATED SUGAR
2	ONIONS, SLICED		PINCH POWDERED CLOVES
1	GREEN PEPPER, SEEDED AND MINCED	1	BAY LEAF
1	29-OZ CAN (3½ C) TOMATOES	1	8-OZ CAN MUSHROOMS AND LIQUID
3	GARLIC CLOVES, FINELY MINCED	1	12-OZ CAN (1⅔ C) WHOLE-KERNEL CORN
1	TBSP WORCESTERSHIRE SAUCE		

Half cover chicken with boiling water, add one sliced onion and simmer, covered, for 2 to 3 hours or until tender. Chill in broth. Remove meat from bones, cutting into pieces of uniform size. Reserve broth for soup or gravy. In a large pan, sauté the remaining onion and green pepper in shortening until tender. Add the tomatoes, garlic, Worchestershire sauce, salt, sugar, cloves, and the bay leaf. Simmer uncovered half an hour, remove the bay leaf, and add the mushrooms (with the liquid) and the corn. Then add the chicken and heat, adding more seasonings if desired.

CHICKEN RUDDERHAM

STEP 1

1	4-LB CHICKEN	1	ONION, QUARTERED
1	CELERY STALK, CHOPPED	1	TSP CAYENNE PEPPER
		1	TBSP SALT

Combine all ingredients and add water to cover. Cook for about 3 hours, or until chicken is tender. Cool, then remove chicken from the liquid. Skin, bone, cut into small pieces, and set aside.

STEP 2

2	TBSP FLOUR	2	C CHOPPED CELERY
3	TBSP BUTTER		SALT AND CAYENNE PEPPER
2	C CHICKEN STOCK		
½	C CHOPPED GREEN BELL PEPPER	1	20-OZ CAN TOMATOES
2	TBSP CHOPPED FRESH PARSLEY	2	TSP CURRY POWDER

Brown flour in butter. Stir in stock. Add green pepper, parsley, and celery. Season to taste with salt and cayenne pepper. Simmer until thickened, adding more flour if necessary. Add the reserved chicken and the tomatoes. Cook over a low flame for 1 hour. Add curry powder, if desired. Serves 8 to 10.

CHICKEN DIVAN PARISIAN

4	LBS (FRESH OR FROZEN) BROCCOLI, COOKED	6	TBSP BUTTER
		4	TBSP FLOUR
		2	C MILK
	SALT AND PEPPER	6	TBSP WHITE WINE
	WHITE MEAT FROM 2 CHICKENS, COOKED	½	LB OLD ENGLISH CHEESE, CUBED

Season broccoli with salt and pepper to taste. Place in the bottom of a greased casserole. Cover with sliced white meat. Melt butter and mix in flour to make a smooth paste. Add milk and cook, stirring until thickened. Add the remaining ingredients and continue cooking until cheese is melted. Pour over chicken and broccoli. Bake at 350°F for 15 minutes, or until heated. Place under broiler flame until top is light brown. Serves 6.

CHICKEN WITH MUSHROOM MARSALA SAUCE

4	BONELESS, SKINLESS CHICKEN BREAST HALVES (ABOUT 6 OZ EACH)	1	LB SMALL WHITE AND/OR CRIMINI MUSHROOMS, SLICED (ABOUT 6 CUPS)
½	TSP SALT	½	C CHOPPED ONION
½	TSP GROUND BLACK PEPPER	1	C MARSALA OR OTHER RED WINE
½	C FLOUR	1	C CHICKEN STOCK
4	TBSP OLIVE OIL		

Season chicken breasts with salt and pepper. Lightly coat both sides of chicken with flour. In a large skillet, heat 2 tablespoons of the olive oil over medium-high heat. Add chicken, cook until golden, about 2 minutes on each side. Transfer to a plate. Reduce heat to medium. Add remaining 2 tablespoons oil to skillet; add mushrooms and onion; cook and stir until tender, about 7 minutes. Stir in Marsala and chicken broth. Return chicken breasts to the pan and simmer, covered, until no pink remains in the center, 10 to 12 minutes. Serves 4.

ROAST DUCK À LA GRAND CHENIER

1	WILD DUCK	½	GARLIC CLOVE,
	BACON DRIPPINGS		MINCED
	SALT AND PEPPER	1	TBSP
	FLOUR		WORCESTERSHIRE
1	SMALL ONION,		SAUCE
	CHOPPED		BOILING WATER

Grease duck with bacon drippings, and sprinkle with salt, pepper, and flour. Stuff cavity with onion, garlic, and Worcestershire sauce. Place in a roasting pan and add boiling water to half the depth of the duck. Pour more drippings over breast. Cover and bake at 275°F for about an hour. Then remove cover and roast for another hour or until browned on all sides, turning duck as necessary. When duck is brown, cover, and finish cooking for another hour or until tender.

DUCK MONTMORENCY

1	4-LB DUCK	½	C DICED ONION
	SALT AND PEPPER TO	2	PTS HOT CHICKEN
	TASTE		STOCK (FRESH OR
1	TBSP BUTTER		CANNED)
½	C DICED CELERY		

MONTMORENCY SAUCE

10	OZ DEMI GLAZE	1	C TART CHERRIES
2	OZ PORT WINE		(FRESH, FROZEN,
4	OZ CURRANT JELLY		OR CANNED)

Separate legs from the duck and cut into four pieces. Cut the breast meat into four pieces. Season with salt and pepper. Brown duck lightly in butter. Add diced celery and onion. Add hot chicken stock. Cover and simmer for 1½ hours. In separate saucepan, heat demi glaze with port wine. Add currant jelly and whole cherries. Stir, simmer for 10 minutes. Place duck on plate (1 piece leg and 1 piece breast per serving). Cover with Montmorency sauce. Serves 4.

CRUNCHY ALMOND TURKEY TOAST

1	LOAF UNCUT WHOLE-WHEAT BREAD	1–2	GARLIC CLOVES, MINCED
2	C COOKED AND CUBED TURKEY	2	TSP FLOUR
4½	TBSP MARGARINE	6	TBSP DRY RED WINE
½	C SLICED ALMONDS	1	C PLAIN LOW-FAT YOGURT
2	TBSP MINCED ONION		FRESH PARSLEY (FOR GARNISH)

Trim end crust from bread. Slice four 1½-inch-thick slices. Pull out center of each slice, leaving about ¼-inch-thick border on all sides including bottom. In a small skillet, melt 1½ tablespoons margarine over low heat. Brush melted margarine around hollow and edges of whole-wheat shells. Toast shells until lightly browned. In 2-quart saucepan, melt remaining 3 tablespoons of margarine over medium heat. Add almonds and onion; stir and cook until both are lightly browned. Stir in garlic and flour; cook, stirring constantly for 1 minute. Remove pan from heat; stir in wine. Return to heat; cook and stir until thickened. Remove pan from heat. Fold in yogurt and turkey; return to heat. Cook until meat is warmed through. Spoon mixture into toast shell. Garnish with parsley. Serve with green vegetable or salad. Serves 4.

RANCH FRIED CHICKEN

1	3½–4 LB FRYER	FLOUR, SEASONED
	MILK TO COVER	WITH SALT AND
	SALT AND PEPPER	PEPPER
	TO TASTE	VEGETABLE OIL
		(FOR DEEP-FRYING)

Cut chicken into serving pieces and remove skin. Soak overnight in milk well seasoned with salt and pepper. One and a half hours before serving, dip chicken in well-seasoned flour and fry in deep fat at 350°F for 20 to 30 minutes, or until brown. Save the milk for gravy.

Drain chicken. Place in a covered roasting pan in a 200°F oven, or in an electric roaster at 150°F, for 30 to 45 minutes. Serves 4 to 6.

BRANDIED QUAIL WITH BREAD SAUCE

6	QUAIL	½	C PORT WINE
	SALT AND PEPPER	1	C RICH CHICKEN
	TO TASTE		OR VEAL STOCK
½	LB BUTTER	1	TBSP CURRANT JELLY
1	C BRANDY		

Rub birds inside and out with salt and pepper and place in small roasting pan. Add butter and roast in 375°F oven for 20 minutes or until tender. Remove from oven. Add brandy, wine, stock, and jelly. Cover tightly and place back in oven for 15 minutes more. Remove from oven. Remove quail from roasting pan. Put sauce back on the stove and allow to gently simmer for 5 minutes. Serve on a bed of wild rice with bread sauce on the side. Serves 6.

BREAD SAUCE

8	SLICES BREAD	1	TSP BUTTER
1½	C HEAVY CREAM	1	TSP SUGAR
2	PINCHES GROUND		
	NUTMEG		

Boil all ingredients together for 2 minutes. Remove from heat and serve.

TURKEY DRESSING

10	C DRIED BREAD	1	TSP PAPRIKA
3	C BROKEN PECANS	4	C MILK
2	LARGE ONIONS,	1	C BUTTER, MELTED
	MINCED	2	EGGS, SLIGHTLY
3	TSP SALT		BEATEN
1	TSP PEPPER	2	C CHOPPED CELERY
3	TSP SAGE		

Put bread through a food processor or roll fine with a rolling pin. Combine with pecans, onions, and seasonings. Stir in remaining ingredients in the order given. If mixture is not as moist as desired, water may be added. This amount will stuff a 14- to 16-pound turkey.

GRILLED HONEY-BARBECUE CHICKEN

4–6 SPLIT CHICKEN
     BREAST HALVES,
     BONE IN

HONEY-BARBECUE CHICKEN SAUCE

1	MEDIUM ONION, FINELY CHOPPED (1 C)	¼	C CLOVER HONEY
¼	C BUTTER OR MARGARINE	2	TBSP LEMON JUICE
1	C KETCHUP	1	TBSP WORCESTERSHIRE SAUCE
⅓	C WATER	¼	TSP PEPPER

Preheat grill to medium-high. Grill chicken over medium-high heat 10 minutes per side to brown slightly. Reduce heat to low (or place chicken over indirect heat) and grill 40 to 50 minutes longer or until internal temperature of chicken reaches 180°F. Meanwhile, in small saucepan sauté onion in butter over medium heat until onion is tender. Stir in remaining ingredients; heat to boil. Reduce heat and simmer, uncovered, 5 minutes. Brush sauce on chicken during last 10 minutes of grilling. Pass remaining sauce. Serves 4 to 6.

PHEASANTS WITH PAPRIKA

¾	C CHOPPED ONION	1	HEAPING TBSP PAPRIKA
½	C BUTTER	1	C SOUR CREAM
2	PHEASANTS, QUARTERED FLOUR (FOR DREDGING)		SALT TO TASTE

Sauté onion in butter in an ovenproof pan until golden. Add pheasants that have been dredged in flour and brown lightly. Sprinkle with paprika. Cover and place in a 275°F oven and bake for 2½ hours. Pour in sour cream. Add salt. Continue to bake for 30 minutes more. Serves 4 to 8.

ROAST WILD DUCK

1	LARGE WILD DUCK	1	TBSP BUTTER
	SALT AND PEPPER	2	TBSP FLOUR
½	APPLE, CHOPPED		GARLIC POWDER,
½	ONION, CHOPPED		SALT, AND PEPPER
1	CELERY STALK,		TO TASTE
	CHOPPED		

Singe duck's pinfeathers and wash cavity well. Sprinkle inside with salt and pepper. Stuff with apple, onion, and celery.

Make a paste by creaming butter and blending in flour, garlic powder, and salt and pepper to taste. Smear over entire exterior of duck. Place in a roaster and cover, without adding any water. Bake at 350°F for 2 hours. Baste frequently during cooking, adding a little water toward the end. Sprinkle breast with paprika if outside crust is slow in browning. Remove stuffing. Serve with spiced apples and wild rice with mushrooms. Serves 2 to 3.

ROAST STUFFED GOOSE

1	GOOSE	2	EGGS
1	LOAF STALE BREAD,		SALT AND PEPPER
	CUBED		TO TASTE
1	LARGE ONION, CUBED	1	DASH POULTRY
2	TBSP MINCED FRESH		SEASONING, IF
	PARSLEY		DESIRED

Wash and clean goose well. Rub inside and out with salt and pepper. Mix well the bread, onion, parsley, and eggs. (No liquid is used in the stuffing because goose is generally fatty.) Season to taste with salt and pepper and poultry seasoning, if used. Stuff goose lightly and place in roaster, breast side down. Cover and roast for 1 hour at 400°F. Remove cover. Turn goose breast side up and continue roasting at 350°F. for 3 hours, uncovered, until nicely browned and tender. Pour off excess fat and make gravy with flour and water thickening. Serves 6 or more.

CAROLINA STUFFING

½ C CHOPPED ONION	½ C STOCK
1 C CHOPPED CELERY	½ C HEAVY CREAM
2 TBSP BUTTER	2 EGGS, WELL BEATEN
2½ C CRUMBLED	SALT AND PEPPER
CORN BREAD	
2 C CHOPPED NUTS	

Sauté onion and celery in butter until soft and transparent. Mix in the remaining ingredients in the order given, adding salt and pepper to taste. If a moist dressing is desired, add a little more stock. Makes enough to stuff a small chicken.

CHICKEN AND DUMPLINGS

1 4–5 LB ROASTING	½ TSP SALT
CHICKEN	½ TSP PEPPER
1 SPANISH ONION,	½ TSP POULTRY
CHOPPED	SEASONING
2 CELERY STALKS,	
CHOPPED	

Boil chicken and remaining ingredients in enough water to cover for 1¼ hours, or until tender.

DUMPLINGS

2 C FLOUR	1¼ C MILK
4 TSP BAKING POWDER	2 TBSP CHOPPED FRESH
½ TSP SALT	PARSLEY

Mix ingredients to form soft dough. Drop with tablespoon into cooked chicken broth. Cook uncovered for 20 minutes.

NEW ORLEANS CHOP SUEY

1½	C UNCOOKED LONG-GRAIN RICE	½	C HOT WATER
3	QTS BOILING WATER	1	3½-LB BOILED CHICKEN
1	TBSP SALT	1	C SLICED MUSHROOMS
1	C CHOPPED CELERY		
1	C MINCED ONION	1½	C COOKED PEAS
⅓	C BUTTER	½	C STUFFED OLIVES
1	TBSP FLOUR		SALT AND PEPPER

Wash rice well. Stir 1 tablespoon salt into boiling water. Gradually add rice and boil briskly for 20 to 25 minutes, or until tender. Drain in a colander, running cold water through it until starchy quality has gone. Steam over simmering water for at least 45 minutes.

Sauté celery and onion in butter until tender and golden. Push vegetables to one side of the pan and smooth in flour. Add hot water and cook vegetables, stirring constantly until blended.

Skin, bone, and chop chicken into half-inch pieces (there should be about 3 cups). Stir into onion mixture together with sliced mushrooms, peas, and olives. Season to taste with salt and pepper. Simmer for 30 minutes, stirring frequently. Spoon generously into individual servings of rice. Serves 6 to 8.

M E A T ★ S

POLENTA WITH SAUSAGES

6	C BOILING WATER		PARMESAN CHEESE
1½	C YELLOW CORNMEAL	1½	C TOMATO SAUCE
½	LB LITTLE SMOKIES		

The day before serving, pour cornmeal into boiling water, stirring constantly to prevent lumps. Put mixture into a double boiler and cook for half an hour. Then pour out on platter to half-inch thickness and let cool. The next day take sausages, prick with fork, and brown in a frying pan. Do not cook too long. Remove from pan, and cut into small pieces. Put sausage in oblong baking dish (earthenware is best). Cut cold polenta meal in squares. Put a layer in the dish, dot with butter and Parmesan cheese, then alternate layers of sausage and polenta, ending with polenta. Pour tomato sauce over all, sprinkle with cheese, and brown in the oven.

BAKED HAM

1	HAM		PREPARED MUSTARD
	SMALL GARLIC PIECES		AS NEEDED
	AS NEEDED	1	BOX LIGHT OR DARK
	WHOLE CLOVES		BROWN SUGAR
	AS NEEDED		BREADCRUMBS
1	BOTTLE WHITE KARO		AS NEEDED
	SYRUP		

Score fat side of ham. Stuff with small pieces of garlic and whole cloves and cover with ham skin or bacon rind to hold in stuffing. Place on a rack in roasting pan, fat side down. Pour Karo syrup over ham and add just enough water to cover rack. Cover and steam 20 minutes to the pound at a low temperature (250° to 325°F), basting every 30 minutes. Remove excess fat and water so as not to let liquid boil upon ham. Let ham cool when done. Remove cloves. Cover fat with mustard and spread brown sugar on top. Cover with breadcrumbs and bake at low temperature (250° to 325°F) for about 45 minutes.

TEXAS RED CHILI

6	OZ SUET, DICED	1	TSP BLACK PEPPER
3	LBS BEEF STEW MEAT, DICED	8	TBSP MASA HARINA (CORN FLOUR)
4	GARLIC CLOVES, CHOPPED	6	C HOT WATER
2	TSP SALT	2	TBSP VINEGAR
5	TBSP CHILI POWDER (OR TO TASTE)	2	TSP BEEF BOUILLON POWDER

Render suet in skillet, remove residue. Sauté meat in fat until lightly browned. Add garlic, salt, chili powder, and pepper. Sprinkle in the masa harina and stir rapidly. Add hot water, vinegar, and bouillon and slowly cook until meat is tender. Serve with side dishes of chopped sweet onion, red kidney beans, shredded sharp cheddar, and canned green chilies (or chopped sweet pepper).

CHICKEN-FRIED STEAK TEXAS STYLE

ROUND STEAK,
   WELL TENDERIZED
   (¼ LB OF RAW MEAT
   PER PERSON)
FLOUR, SEASONED
   WITH SALT AND
   PEPPER

MILK (FOR
   DREDGING)
1 EGG
VEGETABLE OIL
   (FOR FRYING)

Pound flour, salt, and pepper mixture into meat. Add milk to a bowl and beat egg in it. Dip steak in milk and egg mixture, then into flour until well coated. Fry over medium-high heat in about one-half inch of oil until batter is golden brown.

BEEF TENDERLOIN STEAKS WITH ROQUEFORT SAUCE

4 TBSP BUTTER
⅓ C CHOPPED
   SHALLOTS
2 TSP FLOUR
½ C DRY WHITE WINE
⅔ C (ABOUT 3 OZ)
   CRUMBLED
   ROQUEFORT CHEESE

¼ C WHIPPING CREAM
   SALT AND PEPPER
4 (6–8 OZ) BEEF
   TENDERLOIN STEAKS,
   ABOUT 1-INCH THICK

Melt 2 tablespoons butter in heavy saucepan. Add shallots and sauté about 5 minutes. Add flour and stir for 1 minute. Gradually mix in wine. Boil until liquid is reduced to ¼ cup, stirring frequently, for about 5 minutes. Reduce heat to low. Add cheese and stir until melted and smooth. Add ¼ cup cream and simmer until thickened to sauce consistency. Season with salt and pepper.

Melt remaining 2 tablespoons butter in heavy skillet. Season steaks with salt and pepper. Add to skillet and cook until desired doneness, about 5 minutes per side for medium-rare. Transfer steaks to platter. Bring sauce to simmer over low heat. Stir constantly and add more cream if too thick. Stir in any accumulated juices from the steaks. Spoon sauce over the steaks and serve. Serves 4.

TASTY MEAT LOAF

1½	LB GROUND BEEF	1	GARLIC CLOVE,
½	LB GROUND VEAL		MINCED
½	LB GROUND PORK	½	CARROT, GRATED
1	C SALTINE CRACKER	5–8	DRIED SAGE LEAVES,
	CRUMBS (NOT TOO		CRUMBLED
	FINE)		(OR TO TASTE)
2	EGGS		PEPPER TO TASTE
1	LARGE ONION, FINELY	2	C WARM MILK
	CHOPPED	2	STRIPS RAW BACON

Using large bowl, lightly mix meat, crumbs, eggs, onion, garlic, carrot, sage, and pepper. Add warm milk, lifting lightly with a fork to mix. Gently put in greased loaf pan. Do not press down. Top with strips of bacon. Bake uncovered at 375°F for 1½ hours or until brown around the sides. Serves 6 to 8.

BEEF TIPS, TEXAS STYLE

2	LBS SIRLOIN CUT IN	1	TBSP STEAK SAUCE
	1-INCH CUBES	1–2	C WATER
1	TBSP OIL	1	MEDIUM ONION,
1	GARLIC CLOVE,		CHOPPED
	SLASHED	1	JALAPENO, CHOPPED
½	PKG ONION SOUP MIX	2	TBSP CORNSTARCH
1	TBSP TABASCO SAUCE		

Using a 14-inch Dutch oven, brown meat in oil. Add garlic and soup mix. Stir until soup mix dissolves. Add Tabasco, steak sauce, and water. Cook until blended (2 to 3 minutes). Add onion, jalapeno, and cornstarch. Mix well and simmer on low heat for 2 hours.

MEATBALLS

1½	LB GROUND BEEF	⅛	TSP PEPPER
2	TBSP FINELY CHOPPED ONION	½	C MILK
		1	EGG
2	TBSP CHOPPED GREEN BELL PEPPER	¼	C FLOUR
		¼	C SHORTENING
¼	C CORNMEAL	1½	C CANNED OR COOKED TOMATOES, OR TOMATO JUICE
1	TSP CHILI POWDER		
1½	TSP DRY MUSTARD		
1	TSP SALT		

Combine ground beef, onion, green pepper, cornmeal, seasonings, milk, and egg, and blend thoroughly. Form into 12 balls. Roll in flour and brown in hot shortening in skillet. Add remaining flour and tomatoes, cover and bake in 450°F oven for 35 to 45 minutes. Makes 12 meatballs.

BAKED PORK CHOPS

6	LEAN CENTER-CUT PORK CHOPS, ½-INCH THICK	½	C CHOPPED RED BELL PEPPER
		⅛	TSP PEPPER
1	MEDIUM ONION, THINLY SLICED	¼	TSP SALT
			FRESH PARSLEY (FOR GARNISH)
½	C CHOPPED GREEN BELL PEPPER		

Preheat oven to 375°F. Trim fat from pork chops. Place chops in a 13 x 9 inch baking pan. Spread onion and peppers on top of chops. Sprinkle with pepper and salt. Refrigerate for 1 hour. Cover pan and bake 30 minutes. Uncover, turn chops, and continue baking for an additional 15 minutes or until no pink remains. Garnish with fresh parsley. Serves 6.

VEAL CUTLETS WITH SOUR CREAM

2	LBS VEAL CUTLETS FLOUR, SEASONED WITH SALT AND PEPPER	1	4-OZ CAN SLICED MUSHROOMS
1	TSP BUTTER	1	C DRY WHITE WINE
3	TBSP OLIVE OIL	1	C CHICKEN BROTH
1	LARGE ONION, CHOPPED	1	TBSP LEMON JUICE
2	GARLIC CLOVES, MINCED	1	LARGE CONTAINER SOUR CREAM
		2	TBSP FLOUR CHOPPED FRESH PARSLEY (FOR GARNISH)

Dredge veal in flour, salt, and pepper. Heat butter and olive oil in large frying pan. Brown each piece of veal on both sides and set meat aside on plate. Sauté onion, garlic, and drained mushrooms for about 5 minutes. Stir in wine, chicken broth, and lemon juice. Simmer gently for about 15 minutes. Return meat to pan and heat. Mix 2 tablespoons flour in sour cream and stir into meat mixture. Heat only until piping hot. Put in heated serving platter and sprinkle with chopped fresh parsley. Serves 6 to 8.

HUNGARIAN GOULASH (WITH LOTS OF ONIONS)

2	LBS BONELESS RUMP OR ROUND STEAK	1/8	TSP CAYENNE PEPPER
2	TBSP SHORTENING	1	C WATER
3	C THINLY SLICED SWEET ONIONS	3	MEDIUM POTATOES, QUARTERED OR HALVED, DEPENDING ON SIZE
2½	TSP SALT (OR TO TASTE)	½	C CHOPPED GREEN BELL PEPPER
½	TSP PEPPER	1	TSP PAPRIKA
2	TSP PAPRIKA		

Trim excess fat from meat. Cut meat into 1-inch cubes and brown. Add onion—sauté until golden. Add next 5 ingredients. Cover and cook slowly 1½ hours or until meat is almost tender. Add potatoes and green pepper. Cover and cook another 30 minutes. Add remaining paprika. Good with noodles, rice, or mashed potatoes. Serves 6.

BEEF STROGANOFF

1	C BUTTER	3	TBSP TOMATO PASTE
¾	C FLOUR	1	TBSP DRY ENGLISH
1	TSP SALT		MUSTARD
¼	TSP PEPPER	2	TBSP WATER
	DASH CAYENNE	2	C SOUR CREAM
2½	C MILK, SCALDED	2½	LB BEEF TENDERLOIN,
1	MEDIUM ONION,		CUT INTO 2-INCH
	THINLY SLICED		STRIPS
1	C MUSHROOMS	1½	TSP SALT
	JUICE OF 2 LEMONS	¼	TSP PEPPER
1	C DRY WHITE WINE		

Over low heat, melt ¼ cup butter and blend in flour and seasonings. Add milk and cook until thick and smooth. Simmer 10 minutes on low heat. In another pan, over low heat, sauté onion and mushrooms in another ¼ cup butter for about 5 minutes, then add juice of lemons and wine. Reduce the liquid by at least half then add tomato paste and simmer 5 minutes. Stir in mustard blended with water and slowly simmer 5 minutes longer. Remove from heat; blend in sour cream and white sauce. Sauté meat in remaining butter and season with salt and pepper. Blend in sour cream sauce. Heat through but do not boil. Serves 4 to 6.

ROAST LEG OF SPRING LAMB

1	LEG OF SPRING LAMB,		SALT AND PEPPER
	5–6 LBS		TO TASTE
3	GARLIC CLOVES,	4	TBSP MELTED BUTTER
	SLICED LENGTHWISE		JUICE OF 1 LEMON

Wipe leg of lamb with a damp cloth. Make slits with a sharp knife in various places and on both sides of lamb. Insert pieces of garlic in slits made in lamb. Season with salt and pepper and brush with melted butter. Squeeze lemon juice over lamb and place in preheated 450°F oven about ½ hour. Lower heat to moderate, 350° to 375°F, and add 2 cups water. Bake slowly, 20 to 25 minutes per pound, adding more water if needed. Gravy can be made in same pan by removing most of the fat and serving the lamb with its natural gravy.

SAUERBRATEN WITH POTATO DUMPLINGS

3	LBS BEEF POT ROAST	2	TSP SALT
½	C VINEGAR		PEPPER TO TASTE
½	C WATER		FAT OR BACON
1	SMALL ONION, SLICED		DRIPPINGS
2	BAY LEAVES	1	C WATER
3	WHOLE CLOVES		

Place meat in bowl and pour over a mixture of vinegar, water, onion, bay leaves, cloves, salt, and pepper. Cover, refrigerate, and let stand for 18 to 24 hours. Remove meat and brown on all sides with fat or bacon drippings. Over browned meat pour the brine and spices in which it has soaked, adding 1 cup water. Simmer for 3 hours or until tender. Remove meat. Thicken liquid for gravy. Serve with potato dumplings (recipe follows). Serves 6.

POTATO DUMPLINGS

2	C HOT COOKED MASHED POTATOES	1	C ¼-INCH BREAD CUBES, FRIED IN
1	TBSP BUTTER		BACON DRIPPINGS
1	TBSP GRATED ONION		BREADCRUMBS FRIED
1	EGG		IN BUTTER
1½	TSP SALT		
	DASH OF PEPPER		

To hot mashed potatoes add butter. Cool. When cool, add onion and egg. Mix well with fork. Stir in flour, salt, and pepper. Blend well. Make into balls and flatten. Into the center of each place 4 bread cubes fried in bacon drippings. Form balls around these cubes. Place into gently boiling water. Cover tightly and boil for 7 minutes. Lift dumplings and place around sauerbraten in a large platter. Garnish dumplings with breadcrumbs fried in butter.

BURGUNDY OF BEEF

4	LB RUMP ROAST		SALT AND PEPPER
½	C COARSELY CHOPPED		TO TASTE
	CARROTS	6	TBSP BUTTER
½	C COARSELY CHOPPED	2	TBSP FLOUR
	ONIONS	1½	C BEEF STOCK
½	C COARSELY CHOPPED		BURGUNDY WINE
	LEEKS		TO TASTE
½	C COARSELY CHOPPED		
	CELERY		

Place beef on a bed of coarsely chopped carrots, onions, leeks, and celery in an ovenproof pan. Rub beef with seasonings and 3 table-spoons butter. Put in very hot oven and sear the meat well. Then put in Dutch oven. Add 3 tablespoons butter and 2 tablespoons flour to pan, stir until brown, and add beef stock. Pour gravy over beef in Dutch oven. Add Burgundy wine to taste and simmer, covered, until meat is tender. Serves 6 to 8.

APPLE-STUFFED PORK CHOPS

2	TBSP BUTTER OR	¼	C GOLDEN RAISINS
	MARGARINE		SALT AND PEPPER
1	C CHOPPED APPLES		TO TASTE
2	TBSP	1	C SOFT BREADCRUMBS
	WORCESTERSHIRE	1	EGG, BEATEN
	SAUCE	8	PORK CHOPS,
1	C CHOPPED ONIONS		1-INCH THICK
1	C CHOPPED CELERY	¼	C APPLE JELLY

In a large frying pan melt butter or margarine, and add apples, Worcestershire sauce, onion, celery, and raisins. Add salt and pepper, if desired. Sauté until onions are transparent. Remove from heat and add breadcrumbs and egg, mix together. Make a large incision or pocket in the side of each chop. Stuff 1 or 2 tablespoons of sautéed apple mixture into each pocket. Place chops in a large casserole dish, cover, and bake at 375°F for 1 hour.

In a small saucepan melt apple jelly. Remove chops from oven and brush jelly over chops. Return to oven and bake uncovered for 15 more minutes. Serves 8.

LAMB SHANKS

4	LAMB SHANKS	2	CELERY STALKS,
	SALT AND PEPPER		THINLY SLICED
	TO TASTE		LENGTHWISE
2	GARLIC CLOVES,	2	BAY LEAVES, BROKEN
	MINCED	1	TSP DRIED OREGANO
2	SMALL CARROTS, CUT	½	TSP DRIED THYME
	INTO THICK STRIPS	1	C TOMATO SAUCE
1	LARGE ONION,	1	C WATER
	THINLY SLICED	½	C OLIVE OIL
		8	OR MORE NEW
			POTATOES, PEELED

Preheat oven to 375°F. Sprinkle shanks with salt and pepper to taste and rub with garlic. Sprinkle bottom of roasting pan large enough to hold shanks with the carrots, onion, celery, and bay leaves. Add shanks and sprinkle with oregano and thyme. Add tomato sauce diluted with water and the olive oil. Cover tightly. Bake 1½ to 2½ hours depending on size of shanks. If shanks seem to be cooking too quickly, reduce oven heat to 350°F at the end of the first hour of cooking. During the last ½ hour of cooking, raise the temperature of oven to 400°F and uncover the roasting pan. Add potatoes. Serve shanks surrounded by vegetables. Skim off fat from sauce and serve separately. Serves 4.

GINGERED GRILLED LEG OF LAMB

4–5 LB LAMB LEG, WELL-TRIMMED AND BUTTERFLIED	2 JALAPENO PEPPERS, SEEDED
2 TSP SZECHUAN PEPPERCORNS (AVAILABLE AT ASIAN FOOD STORES)	6 GARLIC CLOVES
	1 2-INCH PIECE FRESH GINGER, PEELED
	2 TSP DIJON MUSTARD
2 MEDIUM ONIONS, EACH CUT INTO 8 PIECES	½ C HONEY
	½ C SOY SAUCE
	¼ C VEGETABLE OIL ITALIAN PARSLEY (OPTIONAL)

Place peppercorns in food processor or blender; process 1 minute. Add onions, jalapeno peppers, garlic, ginger, and mustard and puree. Add honey, soy sauce, and oil; process until well blended. Reserve 1 cup. Place lamb in plastic bag, and add remaining marinade, turning to coat. Close bag securely and marinate in refrigerator 6 to 8 hours or overnight, if desired; turn occasionally. Remove lamb from marinade. Thread 2 long metal skewers through lamb to secure and facilitate turning roast. Place lamb on grid over medium coals. Grill 40 to 60 minutes or until desired degree of doneness (140°F for rare, 150°F for medium rare, and 160°F for medium). Turn lamb several times during cooking, brushing with reserved marinade during last 10 minutes of cooking. Let stand 10 minutes. Remove skewers and carve into thin slices. Garnish with parsley, if desired. A butterflied lamb leg will yield four 3-ounce cooked, trimmed servings per pound.

GREEK LAMB

1½ LB LAMB LEG, WELL-
TRIMMED AND
CUT INTO
1½-INCH PIECES
1 C PLAIN YOGURT
1 1.8-OZ ENVELOPE
LEEK OR ONION
SOUP MIX
JUICE OF 1 LIME
1 TBSP WHITE WINE
WORCESTERSHIRE
SAUCE

1 TSP CRUSHED RED
PEPPER PODS
1 RED BELL PEPPER,
CUT INTO 1¼-INCH
PIECES
1 YELLOW BELL PEPPER,
CUT INTO 1¼-INCH
PIECES
6 PITA BREAD ROUNDS
FRESH SPINACH
LEAVES

Combine yogurt, soup mix, lime juice, Worcestershire sauce, and red pepper pods. Place lamb pieces in plastic bag; add marinade, turning to coat. Close bag securely and marinate in refrigerator 3 hours, or overnight, if desired. Turn occasionally. Alternately thread lamb and pepper pieces on each of six 12-inch skewers. Place on grid over medium coals. Grill 15 to 20 minutes, turning occasionally. Place 6 pita rounds on platter and top with spinach leaves. Remove lamb and peppers from skewers onto spinach leaves. Fold pita around lamb to serve. Serves 6.

V E G E T A B L E S

SPANISH HOMINY

1	ONION, CHOPPED	1	8-0Z CAN TOMATOES
1	MEDIUM GREEN BELL	1	8-0Z CAN MUSHROOMS
	PEPPER, CHOPPED	1	C HOMINY, DRAINED
½	TBSP BACON	⅔	LB AMERICAN OR
	DRIPPINGS		CHEDDAR CHEESE,
	CHILI POWDER		GRATED
	TO TASTE		

Brown onion and green pepper in bacon drippings. Add chili powder, tomatoes, and mushrooms, then hominy and cheese. Before serving, if not thick enough, add some breadcrumbs.

SQUASH SOUFFLÉ

1	PKG FROZEN SQUASH,	½	C SUGAR
	DEFROSTED	½	C FLOUR
¼	LB BUTTER, MELTED		DASH OF SALT
2	C MILK OR CREAM		DASH OF GROUND
3	EGGS		CINNAMON

Mix dry ingredients together. Mix squash with melted butter. Beat cream with eggs. Mix all ingredients together in blender or food processor. Pour into greased 2-quart casserole, sprinkle with cinnamon, and bake at 350°F for 1 to 1¼ hours. Serves 2 to 4.

PEAS AND MUSHROOM CASSEROLE

1 8-OZ CAN
MUSHROOMS, OR 1 C
SLICED MUSHROOMS

2 C GREEN PEAS,
COOKED

1 C DICED CELERY

4 HARD-BOILED EGGS,
SLICED

1 C MEDIUM CREAM
SAUCE

1 SMALL ONION,
MINCED

1 TBSP BUTTER

1 CAN CONDENSED
TOMATO SOUP
SALT AND PEPPER
TO TASTE
BUTTERED
BREADCRUMBS

Drain canned mushrooms. If fresh mushrooms are used, wash and scrub them; then sauté them in a little butter until browned. Fill a greased casserole with alternate layers of peas, mushrooms, celery, eggs, and cream sauce (see "Sauces"). Sauté onion in butter until golden. Add soup, salt, and pepper. Pour over mixture in casserole and cover with breadcrumbs. Bake at 450°F for 15 to 20 minutes, or until well heated. Serves 6 to 8.

HOMEMADE BAKED BEANS

2 LBS GREAT
NORTHERN WHITE
BEANS
SALT

1½ C KETCHUP

3 C BROWN SUGAR

½ TSP DRY MUSTARD

3 TBSP
WORCESTERSHIRE
SAUCE
DASH GARLIC
POWDER

2 C RAW DICED BACON

Cook beans in salted water until just tender, about an hour. Mix all ingredients and add to cooked beans. Bake for 3 hours in very slow oven (275°F). Serves 6 to 8.

BEAN BAKE

6	20-OZ CANS CRUSHED PINEAPPLE IN JUICE	6	GREEN BELL PEPPERS, SEEDED AND CHUNKED
12	C COOKED HAM STRIPS	3	C HICKORY SMOKED BARBECUE SAUCE
6	TBSP MARGARINE	2¼	C CHOPPED GREEN ONIONS
3	C CHOPPED YELLOW ONION		
6	20-OZ CANS BAKED BEANS		

Drain pineapple. In nonstick skillet, sauté ham in 2 tablespoons margarine until lightly browned. Add remaining 4 tablespoons margarine and yellow onion. Sauté until onion is soft. Add beans, green pepper, barbecue sauce, green onions, and pineapple. Stir well. Bake in 350°F oven 20 minutes until bubbly. Serves 24.

CORN PUDDING

6	EARS OF CORN	½	TSP PEPPER
2	EGGS, SLIGHTLY BEATEN	2	C MILK
¼	C FLOUR	1½	TBSP BUTTER, MELTED (FOR BAKING DISH)
1	TSP SALT	3	TBSP BUTTER

Take large, tender, milky ears of corn. Husk corn, cut off the tops, and then scrape the cobs well. Add eggs and stir them into the corn. Add flour, salt, and pepper. Stir in milk and mix all together thoroughly. Put into a buttered baking dish about 4 inches deep. Cover the top with butter cut into small pieces. Bake at 350°F for about 1 hour. Serve hot. Serves 4.

GREEN BEAN CASSEROLE

3	C FRENCH-STYLE GREEN BEANS, COOKED	¾	C MILK
		½	LB SHARP CHEESE, CUBED
4	TBSP BUTTER	1	TSP SALT
2	TBSP FLOUR		PAPRIKA TO TASTE

Drain beans well. Place in shallow, greased baking dish. Melt butter over hot water in double boiler. Blend in flour. Mix in milk slowly and cook, while stirring, until thick. Add cheese and salt and continue to cook until smooth. Pour sauce over beans and sprinkle with paprika. Bake at 350°F for 15 minutes, or until thoroughly heated. Serves 6.

CHEESY CARROTS

4	C SLICED, PARBOILED CARROTS	¼	C MILK
1½	C PLAIN CROUTONS	¼	C BUTTER, MELTED
1	C GRATED CHEDDAR CHEESE	1½	TSP WORCESTERSHIRE SAUCE
2	EGGS, BEATEN	1	TSP SALT (OR TO TASTE)

Mix carrots, croutons, and cheese. Put in 1½-quart buttered casserole. Mix remaining ingredients. Pour over carrot mixture. Bake, uncovered, at 400°F for 20 minutes, then serve. Serves 4.

SWEET POTATO SOUFFLE

6	MEDIUM SWEET POTATOES	1	TSP NUTMEG
2	EGG YOLKS, BEATEN	3	TBSP BUTTER, MELTED
½	C MILK	2	EGG WHITES, BEATEN
½	C SUGAR	4	TBSP SUGAR
½	C RAISINS	1	TSP LEMON JUICE OR ORANGE JUICE

Peel potatoes and boil in salted water until tender. Put through a potato ricer or food mill and mash thoroughly. Mix egg yolks, milk, sugar, raisins, nutmeg, and butter and stir in mashed potatoes. Put in buttered casserole and bake in 350°F oven for 30 minutes until light brown on top and bottom. Make a meringue of the egg whites, sugar, and juice and place on top of potatoes. Put under broiler a few minutes to brown. Serves 4 to 6.

SWEET AND SOUR GREEN BEANS

1	LB GREEN BEANS	2	TBSP CIDER VINEGAR
3	SLICES BACON	1	TBSP BROWN SUGAR
2	MEDIUM ONIONS, SLICED	1	TSP SALT
½	TSP DRY MUSTARD	1	C BEAN LIQUID

Cut off tips of beans, string them, and cut them in 1-inch diagonal pieces. Cook in salted water to cover, for about 1 hour or until tender. Drain, reserving 1 cup of liquid.

Fry bacon until crisp. Drain it and cut it into small pieces. Sauté onion in bacon drippings until light brown. Smooth in mustard. Mix in vinegar, brown sugar, salt, and bean liquid. Add beans and bacon. Flavor is greatly improved if the mixture is allowed to stand for an hour or more and then reheated before serving. Serves 4.

HOPPING JOHN

2	C BLACK-EYED PEAS	⅔	BELL PEPPER, CHOPPED
1	HAM BONE		
5	GARLIC CLOVES, CHOPPED	1	20-OZ CAN TOMATOES
			SEVERAL BACON SLICES
1	LARGE ONION, CHOPPED	1½	C UNCOOKED RICE

C ook black-eyed peas with leftover ham bone. Prepare rice according to package directions. Chop garlic, onion, and bell pepper. Divide in half. Add tomatoes and half of the chopped garlic, onion, and pepper to the peas. Cut bacon in small pieces and fry with other half of the garlic, onion, and pepper, then add to peas. Add rice a few minutes before serving. Serve with fried corn pones or hush puppies.

FRIED GREEN TOMATOES

3	LARGE GREEN TOMATOES		SALT AND PEPPER TO TASTE
2	EGGS, BEATEN	2	TBSP BUTTER OR MARGARINE
1	C BREADCRUMBS		

S lice tomatoes thick. Dip into eggs, then into breadcrumbs. Season with salt and pepper. Melt butter or margarine in heavy skillet. When moderately hot, add tomato slices and fry until brown, turning only once. Serve with slices of crisp bacon. (Note: Browning will be accomplished very quickly. Make sure butter or margarine is only moderately hot. If too hot, the egg will cook before the tomatoes are done.)

CANDIED YAMS

3	MEDIUM YAMS (1½ C)	¼	TSP GROUND NUTMEG
¼	C FIRMLY PACKED BROWN SUGAR	¼	TSP GRATED ORANGE PEEL
1	TSP SIFTED FLOUR	1	TSP SOFT TUB MARGARINE
¼	TSP SALT	½	C ORANGE JUICE
¼	TSP GROUND CINNAMON		

Cut yams in half and boil until tender but firm (about 20 minutes). When cool enough to handle, peel and slice into ¼-inch thickness. Combine sugar, flour, salt, cinnamon, nutmeg, and grated orange peel. Place half of the sliced yams in a medium-sized casserole dish. Sprinkle with half of spiced sugar mixture. Dot with half the amount of margarine. Add a second layer of yams, using the rest of the ingredients in the same order as above. Add orange juice. Bake uncovered in preheated 350°F oven for 20 minutes. Serves 6.

SWEET POTATO-CRANBERRY CASSEROLE

2	LBS WHOLE SWEET POTATOES	⅔	C FIRMLY PACKED BROWN SUGAR
1	16-OZ CAN WHOLE-BERRY CRANBERRY SAUCE	⅔	C QUICK-COOKING OATS, UNCOOKED
½	TSP GROUND CINNAMON	¼	C PLUS 2 TBSP MARGARINE OR BUTTER
⅔	C SELF-RISING FLOUR	1	C MINIATURE MARSHMALLOWS

Cook whole sweet potatoes in boiling water to cover 20 minutes or until tender. Let cool to touch. Peel and mash potatoes. Stir in cranberry sauce and cinnamon. Spoon into a lightly greased 2-quart casserole. Combine flour, brown sugar, and oats. Cut in margarine or butter until mixture resembles coarse crumbs. Spoon over sweet potatoes. Bake at 375°F for 20 minutes. Then top with marshmallows and bake just until golden brown. Serves 8.

GREEN BEANS WITH CARAMELIZED ONIONS

4	BACON SLICES, CUT INTO ¼-INCH STRIPS	1	LB FRESH GREEN BEANS, STEMMED AND CUT IN HALF
1	MEDIUM ONION, CUT INTO THIN VERTICAL SLIVERS		SALT AND PEPPER TO TASTE

In a skillet cook bacon until brown and crisp. Remove with a slotted spoon and drain on paper towel; reserve. Pour off all but 1 tablespoon of fat from skillet. Add onion and cook over low heat, stirring often, about 25 minutes. Onion should be tender and slightly golden but not browned. Cook green beans in a microwave or in boiling water until tender; drain. Top with onion and bacon; stir just to combine. Season to taste with salt and pepper. Serves 6.

RANCH VEGETABLES

½–1	LB BUTTER	6	MEDIUM ZUCCHINI, SLICED
5	MEDIUM TO LARGE POTATOES, SLICED WITH SKIN ON	1	BELL PEPPER, SLICED
		2	ONIONS, SLICED
6	MEDIUM YELLOW SQUASH, SLICED		SALT AND PEPPER TO TASTE
		2	TBSP MINCED GARLIC

Melt butter in pan. Put in sliced potatoes with skin and cook for 20 to 30 minutes or until done. Gradually add squash, zucchini, onion, and bell pepper. Add salt and pepper. Add minced garlic. Cover and let simmer over low heat for another 30 minutes to an hour. Serve hot. Serves 10 to 15.

BACON-WRAPPED BAKED POTATO

MEDIUM-SIZE POTATO
SALT AND PEPPER
1 TBSP BUTTER PER
POTATO

2 BACON SLICES PER
POTATO

Use medium-size baking potatoes. Split while raw (do not cut all the way through the potato). Season with butter, salt, and pepper. Place one slice of raw bacon in middle of potato. Wrap tightly in foil. Bake at 350°F for one hour or until tender when pierced with a fork. When done, remove the bacon and wrap with a cooked piece of crispy bacon. Serve immediately.

MACARONI AND TOMATOES

2 C UNCOOKED
MACARONI
1 ONION, CHOPPED
2 TBSP BACON
DRIPPINGS

2 20-OZ CANS
TOMATOES, MASHED
SALT AND PEPPER
TO TASTE

Cook macaroni according to directions. Pour off water. Sauté onion in bacon drippings. Add tomatoes, salt, and pepper. Add cooked macaroni. Simmer gently for 10 minutes.

CORN FRITTERS

1 TBSP SUGAR
1 C FLOUR, SIFTED
1 TSP SALT
1 TBSP SALAD OIL
2 EGGS, BEATEN
1 TSP BAKING POWDER

1 C MILK
1 C CANNED WHOLE
KERNEL CORN
HONEY
VEGETABLE OIL
(FOR DEEP-FRYING)

Mix all ingredients together and drop by small spoonful into deep hot oil heated to 360°F. Fry until golden brown, drain on paper towels, and serve with honey. Makes about 12 fritters.

DOWN HOME GREEN BEANS WITH HAM

1	SLICE COUNTRY-STYLE HAM	1	16-OZ CAN WHOLE GREEN BEANS, DRAINED WITH LIQUID RESERVED
1	TBSP BACON DRIPPINGS		TABASCO SAUCE TO TASTE
½	SMALL ONION, COARSELY CHOPPED		SALT TO TASTE
½	C WATER		

In skillet, cook ham in bacon drippings over high heat and brown on both sides. Cut browned ham into pieces and set aside. Lower heat, add onion, and cook until transparent. Add water a little at a time to prevent splattering. Add beans, reserved liquid, Tabasco sauce, and ham and bring to a simmering boil. Cook for 25 minutes. Remove pan from heat and let beans steep 10 minutes more. Season with salt. Serve hot.

POTATO CASSEROLE

2	LBS FROZEN HASH BROWN POTATOES	1	PT SOUR CREAM WITH CHIVES
½	C BUTTER, MELTED	½	C CHOPPED ONION
1	TSP SALT	½	C CHOPPED CELERY
¼	TSP PEPPER	2	C GRATED CHEDDAR CHEESE
1	CAN CREAM OF POTATO SOUP OR CREAM OF CHICKEN SOUP		

Defrost potatoes. Combine melted butter, salt, pepper, soup, and sour cream. Mix hash browns with onion, celery, and cheese. Mix in soup mixture. Pour into a greased 9 x 12-inch casserole dish. Top with the following mixture.

TOPPING

2	C CRUSHED POTATO CHIPS	½	C BUTTER, MELTED

Mix butter and chips. Sprinkle on top of casserole. Bake 45 minutes at 350°F. Serves 16. This dish can be frozen and heated before serving.

HEALTHY POTATO WEDGES OR FRENCH FRIES

4   POTATOES (3½ OZ   SALT-FREE SEASONING
     EACH)*   TO TASTE
2   EGG WHITES,
     UNBEATEN

Preheat oven to 425°F. Cut potatoes into wedges. For french fries, cut into thin slices. Dip wedges (or fries) into unbeaten egg whites and place on a nonstick pan sprayed with vegetable spray. Season with salt-free seasoning and bake 25 minutes for wedges, 20 minutes for french fries, or until golden brown. Serves 4.

*A combination of brown and sweet potatoes is delicious.

COWBOY BEANS

1   LB RED OR   2   MEDIUM ONIONS,
       PINTO BEANS   WHOLE
1½   QTS WATER   2   THIN SLICES OF
⅛   LB SALT PORK   JALAPENO PEPPER
3   TBSP BROWN SUGAR   SALT TO TASTE
2   GARLIC CLOVES,   1   16-OZ CAN TOMATOES
       SLASHED

Put beans, water, salt pork, and brown sugar in Dutch oven. Cook for 2 hours on low heat. Add garlic, onions, jalapeno pepper, and salt. Cook for 1 more hour until juicy and tender, then add tomatoes. Simmer for 20 minutes. Serve piping hot from Dutch oven. Serves 6 cowboys.

DOWN HOME SPICY HOT BEANS

1	16-OZ PKG DRIED PINTO BEANS	½	C WORCESTERSHIRE SAUCE
6	C WATER	1	TBSP BROWN SUGAR
1	LB BACON SLICES, CUT IN HALF	2	TBSP GROUND CUMIN
1	LB SMOKED BEEF SAUSAGE LINKS	1	TBSP PEPPER
		1	TBSP CELERY SEEDS
2	MEDIUM ONIONS, CHOPPED	2–3	TSP HOT PEPPER SAUCE
½	C CHOPPED GREEN BELL PEPPER	1	TSP SALT
		1	BAY LEAF
4	GARLIC CLOVES, MINCED	1	16-OZ CAN TOMATOES, UNDRAINED AND CHOPPED

Sort and wash beans. Place in large Dutch oven. Cover with water 2 inches above beans. Let soak 3 hours. Drain beans and return to Dutch oven. Add 6 cups water. Combine bacon and next four ingredients in a skillet. Cook over medium heat until bacon is done and vegetables are tender. Drain. Add vegetables and remaining ingredients except tomatoes to the beans and bring mixture to a boil. Cover, reduce heat, and simmer (medium low) for 2 hours or until beans are tender. Stir occasionally. Add tomatoes. Cook 30 minutes longer. Remove bay leaf before serving. Serves 10.

ONION RINGS

3	SPANISH ONIONS, PEELED AND SLICED	¾	TSP SALT
			FLOUR
2	EGGS, LIGHTLY BEATEN	1	C BREADCRUMBS
			VEGETABLE OIL
2	TBSP MILK		(FOR DEEP-FRYING)

Slice onions into rings ¼ inch thick. Place in ice-cold water for 20 minutes. Drain onions and dry on absorbent paper. Beat eggs with milk and salt. Dip onions in flour, then in egg mixture, return to flour, then to egg mixture again. Roll in fresh breadcrumbs (dry breadcrumbs may be used but fresh ones are better). Fry in deep hot oil (370°F). Drain on absorbent paper.

TEXAS CABBAGE

2	C COOKED RICE	2	16-OZ CANS TOMATO SAUCE WITH HERBS
1	LB GROUND BEEF		
1	HEAD CABBAGE, SHREDDED	2	TSP SALT (OR TO TASTE)
½	C DICED ONION	4	TSP CHILI POWDER
2	PKGS POWDERED BEEF OR CHICKEN BOUILLON	½	TSP PEPPER
		½	TSP GARLIC POWDER
		½	LB CHEDDAR CHEESE, GRATED

In nonstick skillet, brown ground beef. In casserole dish, combine meat with cooked rice and 1 package of bouillon. Add salt, chili powder, pepper, and garlic powder. Mix well. Layer cabbage on top of meat and rice; sprinkle onions over cabbage. Sprinkle second package of bouillon on top. Cover with herbed tomato sauce. Cover casserole and bake in 350°F oven 45 minutes. Remove cover, add cheddar cheese, and continue baking just to melt cheese. Cheese should be just melted, not browned. Serve piping hot from casserole. Serves 6.

CRUNCHY BAKED TOMATOES

4	LARGE RIPE TOMATOES	¼	C MARGARINE, MELTED
½	C GRATED SHARP CHEDDAR CHEESE	¾	TSP DRIED BASIL, CRUMBLED
½	C DRY BREADCRUMBS	⅛	TSP CAYENNE PEPPER
½	C PEANUTS, ROASTED AND CHOPPED		

Wash and cut tomatoes in half and place cut side up in a baking dish. In a small bowl combine cheese, breadcrumbs, peanuts, melted margarine, basil, and cayenne pepper. Blend well. Spoon approximately 1 heaping tablespoon of cheese mixture on top of each tomato half. Bake in preheated 350°F oven until topping is golden (about 15 minutes).

DILLY TURKEY-STUFFED TOMATOES

6 MEDIUM TOMATOES

2 C COOKED AND CUBED TURKEY

1 C GRATED ZUCCHINI (1 SMALL)

⅓ C SLICED GREEN ONIONS

¼ C CHOPPED CELERY (1 STALK)

⅓ C CHOPPED GREEN BELL PEPPER

3 TBSP MINCED FRESH PARSLEY

2 TBSP MINCED FRESH DILL (ABOUT 1 TBSP DRIED)

¼ TSP GARLIC POWDER

¼ TSP PEPPER

¼ C REDUCED-CALORIE MAYONNAISE

SPRIGS OF FRESH DILL (FOR GARNISH)

LETTUCE LEAVES (FOR GARNISH)

Cut tops from tomatoes. Scoop out pulp and seeds; discard. Turn tomatoes upside down on paper towel to drain. In medium bowl combine remaining ingredients except dill and lettuce; cover and refrigerate for 1 or 2 hours or overnight. To serve, fill tomato shells with turkey mixture. If desired, garnish with a sprig of fresh dill and serve on lettuce leaf. Serves 6.

RANCH BAKED BEANS

1 LARGE CAN (1 LB 14 OZ) PORK AND BEANS

¼ LB RAW BACON, DICED

1 C KETCHUP

½ C BROWN SUGAR

¼ TSP GROUND CINNAMON

¼ TSP GROUND CLOVES

¼ TSP GROUND GINGER

½ C WATER

Mix all together and bake in casserole dish for 1½ hours at 300°F. Serves 6 to 8.

ONION TART

2	LARGE SWEET ONIONS, PEELED, SLICED, AND SEPARATED INTO RINGS	2	TBSP MINCED FRESH CHIVES
		1	C SKIM MILK
		¼	C EGG SUBSTITUTE
		2	EGG WHITES
1½	TSP OLIVE OIL	1	TSP SAGE

Heat olive oil in a 10-inch overnproof skillet; add onions and chives. Cook slowly over low heat until onions are soft, approximately 3 minutes. In a bowl, whisk together milk, egg substitute, egg whites, and sage. Pour egg mixture over onions and bake in 325°F oven until set, approximately 30 minutes. Slice into 4 wedges. Serve warm. Serves 4.

CHEESY POTATOES OLÉ

6	MEDIUM POTATOES, PEELED AND SLICED ¼-INCH (ABOUT 4 C) SALT AND PEPPER TO TASTE	1	C SOUR CREAM
		½	C BACON (ABOUT 8 SLICES), COOKED AND CRUMBLED
1	1¼-OZ PKG TACO SEASONING MIX	2	C SHREDDED SHARP CHEDDAR CHEESE
¾	C MILK	½	C FINE CRUMBS (BREAD, CRACKER, OR CORN FLAKES)

Cook potatoes until just tender. Drain and arrange in buttered shallow ovenproof casserole. Season potatoes with salt and pepper. Combine taco seasoning, milk, and sour cream; beat until smooth. Stir in bacon and pour over potatoes. Sprinkle with cheese and crumbs. Bake uncovered at 350°F for 30 to 40 minutes. Serves 6 to 8.

MEXICAN FOOD

CHICKEN TAMALE PIE

1   3–5 LB CHICKEN,
    STEWED
3   TBSP CHILI POWDER
2   20-OZ CANS CREAMED
    CORN

    CHICKEN STOCK
2   1-LB, 2-OZ CANS
    TAMALES

Pull meat off chicken bones in large pieces. Place a layer of chicken in a greased casserole. Sprinkle with some of the chili powder. Cover with a layer of tamales and more chili powder, then with a layer of corn and chili powder. Repeat until all ingredients are used. Add just enough juice from the tamales and chicken stock to cover. Bake at 300°F for 1 hour. Serves 8.

CHILI SAUCE

6   LARGE RIPE
    TOMATOES
2   C VINEGAR
1   BAG PICKLING SPICE
6   MEDIUM ONIONS
3   LARGE GREEN
    BELL PEPPERS

2   LARGE RED BELL
    PEPPERS
1   HOT RED PEPPER
1   TSP GROUND CLOVES
1   STICK CINNAMON
2   C BROWN SUGAR
    SALT TO TASTE

Peel tomatoes. Cook until tender; then add 2 cups vinegar and the remaining ingredients. Cook down until thick. Bottle while hot.

MEXICAN MACARONI

1	LARGE ONION, CHOPPED	1	C COLD WATER
1	LB GROUND ROUND STEAK	1	16-OZ CAN TOMATOES
	PAPRIKA, SALT, AND	¾	C DICED CELERY
	PEPPER TO TASTE	1	BAY LEAF
1	TBSP FLOUR	¼	C FRESH CHOPPED PARSLEY
		1	C MACARONI

Cook chopped onion in butter; add meat, paprika, salt, and pepper; cook until almost done. Add flour and cold water and cook until meat is tender. Add tomatoes, celery, and bay leaf, and cook until well done. Add parsley about 5 or 10 minutes before serving; remove bay leaf. Cook macaroni until tender. Make mold of macaroni in center of plate and pour meat mixture around it. Sprinkle paprika freely for garnish.

CHALUPAS

1	LB GROUND BEEF	1	10½-OZ CAN TOMATO SOUP
2	MEDIUM ONIONS, CHOPPED	1	3-OZ CAN EVAPORATED MILK
2	TBSP BACON DRIPPINGS		SALT TO TASTE
2	TBSP FLOUR		GRATED CHEDDAR CHEESE TO TASTE
2–3	TBSP CHILI POWDER	12	TORTILLAS

Sauté beef and one of the onions in bacon drippings until brown, sprinkling with flour and chili powder during cooking. Add water to cover and simmer for 30 minutes.

Combine tomato soup, milk, cheese, and the remaining onion, and season with salt. Cut up tortillas. Cover the bottom of a greased baking dish with a layer of tortillas, then a layer of meat, and top with cheese mixture. Repeat until all ingredients are used, ending with cheese. Bake at 325°F for about 40 minutes or until cheese has melted and browned. The meat mixture may be made the day before serving. Serves 6.

GUACAMOLE

2	SMALL RIPE TOMATOES, PEELED	1	TSP SALT
1	LARGE ONION, PEELED AND QUARTERED	1	TSP DRIED RED CHILI PEPPERS WITH SEEDS (OR 6 DASHES TABASCO)
3	VERY RIPE AVOCADOS, PEELED AND PITTED		

P ut tomatoes and onions through a food grinder, using the fine blade. Set aside to drain well. Just before serving, mash avocado to a pulp with a fork. Add salt and dried pepper. Mix in onions and tomatoes thoroughly. Serve with toasted tortillas.

FRIJOLES

1	LB DRIED PINTO BEANS	1	GARLIC CLOVE
½	TSP SALT	8	TBSP BACON DRIPPINGS

C over beans with cold water. Add salt and garlic. Simmer for about 3½ hours, or until tender. Cool in liquid. Drain, reserving liquid.

Heat 2 tablespoons of the bacon drippings in a skillet. Add ½ cup of beans that have been mashed. Cook slowly, while stirring, until drippings are mixed in well. Add a little more dripping and more mashed beans, repeating until all are used. Stir in salt to taste. If beans seem dry, add a little water to moisten. Serves 4 to 6.

ENCHILADAS

24	SOFT TORTILLAS		SALT AND PEPPER
2	TBSP OIL		TO TASTE
1	GARLIC CLOVE,		CHOPPED RAW
	MINCED		ONION (FOR
½	C CHOPPED ONION		FILLING)
1	TBSP CHILI POWDER		GRATED MOZZARELLA
1	C TOMATO PUREE		CHEESE (FOR
½	C BEEF OR CHICKEN		FILLING AND
	STOCK		TOPPING)
1	TSP GROUND CUMIN		

Preheat oven to 350°F. In heavy saucepan, heat oil. When hot, add garlic and onion and sauté until golden, then add chili powder, tomato puree, and stock. Stir, then season with cumin, salt, and pepper. Spread this sauce over the tortillas and fill centers of each with desired quantities of chopped raw onion and chopped mozzarella cheese. Roll the tortillas and place in an ovenproof dish. Pour more sauce over the rolled tortillas and sprinkle with more cheese. Bake for 12–15 minutes until thoroughly heated. Serve immediately. Makes 2 dozen.

TACOS

1	ONION, CHOPPED	3	GREEN CHILES,
2	TBSP BUTTER		PEELED AND
½	C TOMATO JUICE		CHOPPED
	DASH THYME		(OR ½ C CANNED
	SALT TO TASTE		CHILES)
	DASH CAYENNE		PREPARED TACO
1	C CHOPPED COOKED		SHELLS
	MEAT (CHICKEN,		SHREDDED LETTUCE
	PORK SAUSAGE,		(FOR GARNISH)
	OR GROUND BEEF)		

Sauté onion in butter until golden brown. Add other ingredients and simmer for 3 minutes. Fill taco shells and place in hot oven only until shells are piping hot. Just before serving, sprinkle shredded cold crisp lettuce atop each taco.

GREEN CHILE ENCHILADAS

12	LARGE GREEN CHILES	2	C COARSELY GRATED MILD AMERICAN CHEESE
2	C COARSELY CHOPPED ONIONS		
2	TBSP SHORTENING	4	C HEAVY CREAM
2	C CANNED TOMATOES, DRAINED	18	TORTILLAS
	SALT AND PEPPER TO TASTE	1	LARGE ONION, MINCED
		¼	LB MILD AMERICAN CHEESE, FINELY GRATED

Wash and dry chiles. Place them under the broiler, turning once or twice to blister skin. Remove from broiler and lay them on half of a damp cloth and cover with the other half. When cool enough to handle, peel. Cut off stems; make one slit in each chile and remove seeds, leaving the veins intact. Chop coarsely and measure. There should be about 2 cups.

In bottom of a heavy saucepan, sauté onion in shortening until transparent, and add chiles, tomatoes, salt, and pepper. Cook for 30 to 40 minutes, stirring occasionally, until chiles are very tender. Mix in cheese and simmer, stirring constantly, until cheese is melted.

Turn off fire and stir in cream. Cook over a low flame for a few minutes until heated. Add more salt if necessary. Keep mixture warm while preparing tortillas. If sauce thickens too much, add a little more cream.

Heat about one-half inch of fat in a skillet. Working with one at a time, fry tortillas for a minute in very hot fat, turning once. Do not get them too crisp to bend. As each is fried, dip it in the sauce and lay it in a shallow, greased pan. Place 1 heaping teaspoon onion and 1 heaping teaspoon cheese along the center of each. Fold two opposite ends over stuffing to make a cylinder. Lay enchiladas side by side and pour sauce over all. Sprinkle with any leftover cheese. Bake at 350°F for about 10 minutes, or until well heated. Serve with a side dish of the remaining sauce. Serves 6.

MEXICAN CASSEROLE

1	20-OZ CAN CHILI CON CARNE
½	20-OZ CAN RANCH STYLE BEANS, DRAINED
1	C LARGE ONIONS, SLICED
1	4-OZ BAG CORN CHIPS
½	C GRATED NEW YORK CHEESE

Grease 1½-quart casserole. Fill it with thin layers of chili, beans, onions, and corn chips. Have chili as the top layer. Sprinkle with cheese. Bake at 400°F for about 45 minutes, or until heated and browned. Serves 4.

ARROZ CON POLLO

1	2½–3 LB FRYER
¼	C OLIVE OIL
3	MEDIUM YELLOW ONIONS
2	PIMIENTOS
1	GREEN BELL PEPPER
1	LARGE GARLIC CLOVE
1½	C CANNED TOMATOES
8–10	JUMBO SHRIMP, COOKED
4	C BOILING STOCK
1	TBSP SALT
½	TSP PEPPER
1	TSP SAFFRON
2	BAY LEAVES
1	C UNCOOKED RICE
1	TBSP BUTTER

Clean and cut chicken into serving pieces. Brown in olive oil. Remove from pan and place in a kettle. Then peel and slice onions; clean and chop pimientos and green pepper; mince garlic; and sauté all ingredients until soft in the oil remaining in the skillet.

Add onion mixture, tomatoes, shrimp, broth (made by boiling giblets and neck in water for 30 minutes), and seasonings to chicken. Cover and simmer for 20 minutes.

Brown rice lightly in butter, then mix into chicken. Cover and cook, without stirring, for 30 to 45 minutes, or until chicken is done and rice is tender and dry. Serves 6 to 8.

TAMALE PIE

1	20-OZ CAN CORN	1	LB GROUND BEEF
1	20-OZ CAN TOMATOES		SALT AND PEPPER
1½	C CORNMEAL		TO TASTE
½	C SHORTENING	4	TSP CHILI POWDER
1	ONION, CHOPPED	½	9-OZ CAN RIPE
2	GARLIC CLOVES,		OLIVES, DRAINED
	CHOPPED		AND SLICED
1	GREEN BELL PEPPER,		(OPTIONAL)
	CHOPPED		

Combine corn and tomatoes in a saucepan. Bring to a boil while stirring. Gradually add cornmeal. Cook for a few minutes until thick, stirring constantly. Sauté onion, garlic, and green pepper in shortening until onion is golden. Add beef, salt, pepper, chili powder, and olives. Cook for 5 minutes. Blend in corn mixture and place in a greased casserole. Bake at 300°F for 1½ to 2 hours. Serves 8.

TOSTADAS, TEXAS STYLE

10	TORTILLAS	1½	C SHREDDED ICEBERG
	OIL (FOR FRYING)		LETTUCE
2	RIPE AVOCADOS,	10	THIN ROAST BEEF
	PEELED AND MASHED		SLICES, CUT INTO
½	C MAYONNAISE		1-INCH STRIPS
3	TBSP FINELY	1	MEDIUM TOMATO,
	CHOPPED ONION		CHOPPED
1	TSP LEMON JUICE	1½	C (6 OZ) GRATED
¼	TSP SALT		MONTEREY JACK
	DASH OF HOT		CHEESE
	PEPPER SAUCE		

Fry tortillas in ¼-inch hot oil until crisp and golden, turning once; drain well. Combine avocados, mayonnaise, onion, lemon juice, and seasonings; mix well. Spread tortillas with avocado mixture; top with remaining ingredients. Serves 10.

CHILE RELLENO CASSEROLE

1	27-OZ CAN MILD WHOLE GREEN CHILES	3	EGGS
		3	TBSP FLOUR
1	LB MONTEREY JACK CHEESE	1	5-OZ CAN EVAPORATED MILK
1	LB LONGHORN CHEESE	1	15-OZ CAN TOMATO SAUCE

P reheat oven to 350°F. Wash and split the chiles. Remove any seeds or skin. Lay flat on paper towels to dry. Grate cheeses, reserving ¼ cup of each for topping. Layer chiles flat in a 9 x 13-inch baking dish; follow with layers of cheeses. Repeat layers of chiles and cheeses. Beat together eggs, flour, and evaporated milk. Pour evenly over dish. Bake, uncovered, for 30 minutes. Remove from oven and let cool. When cool, pour tomato sauce over top. Sprinkle with reserved cheeses and return to oven; bake 15 minutes. Serves 8.

TACO SALAD

1	1¼-OZ PKG TACO SEASONING MIX	2	C CHOPPED TOMATOES
¾	C MAYONNAISE OR SALAD DRESSING	½	C PITTED RIPE OLIVE HALVES
1	LB GROUND BEEF	½	C (2 OZ) SHREDDED MILD CHEDDAR CHEESE
¾	C WATER		
3	C SHREDDED LETTUCE		

C ombine 2 teaspoons seasoning mix and mayonnaise; chill. Brown meat; drain well. Add remaining seasoning mix and water; simmer 15 minutes, stirring occasionally. Let cool. Cover serving platter with lettuce. Top with tomatoes, olives, meat mixture, cheese, and mayonnaise mixture. Serve with tortilla chips. Serves 4.

RANCH HAND MEXICAN PIE

	ENOUGH PREPARED MASHED POTATOES FOR 4 SERVINGS	2–3	TSP CHILI POWDER (OR TO TASTE)
1	EGG, SLIGHTLY BEATEN	¼	TSP SALT
¼	C SLICED GREEN ONIONS (WITH TOPS)	¼	TSP GARLIC POWDER
1	LB GROUND BEEF	1	C SHREDDED CHEDDAR OR MONTEREY JACK CHEESE
½	C ONION, CHOPPED		
1	8-OZ CAN TOMATO SAUCE		SOUR CREAM, GREEN BELL PEPPER, TOMATO, AND AVOCADO (FOR GARNISH)
¼	C SLICED RIPE OLIVES		

Heat oven to 425°F. Grease 9-inch pie plate. Place mashed potatoes in a bowl, stir in egg and green onions. Spread and press potato mixture evenly against bottom and side of pie plate. Bake 20 to 25 minutes or until light brown. Cook ground beef and chopped onion in 10-inch skillet, stirring occasionally, until beef is brown; drain thoroughly. Stir in remaining ingredients except cheese. Cover and cook over low heat 5 minutes, stirring occasionally. Spoon into shell; sprinkle with cheese. Bake 2 to 3 minutes or until cheese is melted. If desired, garnish with sour cream, green bell pepper, tomato, and avocado. Serves 4.

S A L A D S

CALICO COLESLAW

1	EXTRA-LARGE HEAD GREEN CABBAGE	1	C ALMONDS, BLANCHED AND SLIVERED
1	SMALL RED CABBAGE		
3	APPLES, PEELED AND FINELY CUT	1½	C CANNED PINEAPPLE, FINELY CUT
		1½	C MAYONNAISE

Cut a slice off the large cabbage. Hollow out cabbage with a sharp knife, making a shell 1 inch thick. Wash well with cold water and invert to drain. Keep in a cold place until ready to serve.

Chop the insides, which have been removed, and the small red cabbage very fine, discarding the heart. Wash well and drain thoroughly. Combine cabbage, apples, almonds, pineapple, and mayonnaise. Pile into the cabbage shell and serve. There will be enough slaw to refill the shell once. Serves 8 to 10.

GERMAN POTATO SALAD

6	LARGE POTATOES, COOKED	½	C CHOPPED ONION
		½	C CHOPPED CELERY

Peel and cube potatoes while hot. Add onion and celery. Cover with the following hot dressing.

HOT DRESSING

6	BACON SLICES, FINELY CUT	½	C WATER
3	TBSP SUGAR	2	EGGS, SLIGHTLY BEATEN
2	TBSP FLOUR	1	TSP SALT
½	C VINEGAR		PEPPER TO TASTE

Fry bacon until crisp. Remove from pan and drain, reserving drippings. In a separate bowl, combine sugar and flour. Gradually add vinegar, water, eggs, and seasonings. Blend thoroughly. Mix into bacon drippings and cook until thickened. Add bacon. Serves 8.

BEAN SALAD

1	C CUT CANNED GREEN BEANS	½	C FINELY CHOPPED ONION
1	C DARK RED KIDNEY BEANS	½	C FINELY CHOPPED CELERY
1	C CUT WAX BEANS	½	C FRENCH DRESSING
1	GARLIC CLOVE	½	C MAYONNAISE
		1	HEAD LETTUCE

Drain juices off and chill beans thoroughly. Rub mixing bowl with garlic. Add onion, celery, and mixed beans to the bowl. Mix with equal parts of French dressing and mayonnaise. Serve on chilled lettuce leaves. Serves 4.

SHRIMP AND NECTARINE SALAD CAPRI

3 LBS DRY FETTUCCINE (6 QTS COOKED)	1 LB ONIONS, CUT IN WEDGES (ABOUT 3 C)
6 LBS LARGE PRAWNS	6 LBS FRESH NECTARINES, PITTED AND CUT IN WEDGES
1 1-LB GREEN BELL PEPPER, CUT IN 1-INCH CUBES (ABOUT 4½ CUPS)	6 LBS FRESH SALAD GREENS

Cook fettuccine according to package directions. Drain and cool. Marinate prawns, peppers, onions, and nectarines in 3 cups nectarine dressing (recipe follows) for 15 minutes. Thread onto 72 (6-inch) skewers and broil. Arrange greens on individual salad plates. Top with 1 cup fettuccine and lay 3 broiled skewers on top of each salad. Serve with additional dressing on the side for dipping or drizzle over all.

NECTARINE DRESSING

3¾ LB FRESH NECTARINES, PITTED AND CHOPPED	¾ C FRESH LEMON JUICE
2 TBSP FINELY CHOPPED ONION	¾ C FRESH LIME JUICE
1 C WATER	¾ C RICE VINEGAR SALT TO TASTE
1½ C SUGAR	¼ C SALAD OIL

In saucepan, combine nectarines, onion, and water. Bring to boil; reduce heat; cover and simmer for 5 minutes. Remove from heat, cool, and puree. Return to saucepan; stir in remaining ingredients. Return to boil; simmer 10 minutes. Cool. Serves 24.

BARLEY SALAD

1	C UNCOOKED QUICK BARLEY	¼	C CHOPPED GREEN ONION
2	C COOKED AND CHOPPED TURKEY	1	8-OZ CARTON ORANGE YOGURT
2	TBSP SOY SAUCE	2	C THINLY SLICED CELERY
1	C HALVED GREEN GRAPES	1	TSP SUGAR
1	11-OZ CAN MANDARIN ORANGES		

Cook barley according to package directions. Drain. Cool. Combine remaining ingredients and chill. Serve on lettuce leaves or a melon half. Serves 8.

BLUEBERRY-ORANGE ONION SALAD

1	LARGE ORANGE, THINLY SLICED		SALAD GREENS AS NEEDED
1	LARGE SWEET ONION, THINLY SLICED	1	C FRESH BLUEBERRIES

Arrange thinly sliced orange and onion over salad greens. Place fresh blueberries on top. Serve with blueberry blue cheese dressing. Serve at room temperature. Serves 4.

BLUEBERRY BLUE CHEESE DRESSING

1	C OLIVE OIL	1	C FRESH BLUEBERRIES
⅓	C BLUEBERRY VINEGAR		SALT AND PEPPER TO TASTE
2	TBSP CRUMBLED BLUE CHEESE		

In a large screw-top jar, combine olive oil, vinegar, blue cheese, blueberries, salt, and pepper. Shake until well blended. Serve at room temperature. Can be stored in refrigerator.

CARROT-RAISIN SALAD

4	MEDIUM CARROTS, SHREDDED	2	TSP SUGAR
¼	C RAISINS		JUICE OF 1 LEMON

I n a medium bowl, thoroughly mix carrots, raisins, sugar, and lemon. Serve chilled. Serves 4.

FRUIT SALAD WITH CREAMY LIME DRESSING

2	KIWI	1	PT STRAWBERRIES
1	PT FRESH BLUEBERRIES		

W ash fruit. Peel and slice kiwi. Using the tip of a paring knife, cut the entire kiwi into a fun star shape, then slice it into ¼-inch pieces. Remove green caps from strawberries and slice in half. Combine with blueberries and kiwi in a serving bowl. Cover and refrigerate. Carefully stir in creamy lime dressing just before serving. Serves 6.

CREAMY LIME DRESSING

⅓	C SOUR CREAM	1	TSP LIME ZEST
1½	TBSP HONEY	¼	TSP SALT
2	TBSP FRESH LIME JUICE	1	TBSP CHOPPED FRESH MINT LEAVES

I n a small bowl combine all ingredients; refrigerate at least 1 hour before serving.

AMBROSIA FRUIT AND NUT MOLD

2	3-OZ PACKAGES LIME GELATIN	1	SMALL CAN CRUSHED PINEAPPLE, UNDRAINED
2½	C BOILING WATER	1	PT SOUR CREAM
1	SMALL JAR MARASCHINO CHERRIES, CHOPPED	½	C WALNUTS

Dissolve lime gelatin in water. Set aside; when thoroughly cooled, add sour cream and mix well with mixer on slowest speed. Fold in rest of ingredients. Pour into greased mold and refrigerate for one hour. When ready to serve, place mold in pan of warm water briefly to loosen and then turn into a serving dish. Serves 4 to 6.

GREEN SALAD WITH GORGONZOLA CHEESE DRESSING

½	LB GORGONZOLA CHEESE, CHOPPED	4–5	GREEN ONIONS
½	C SALAD OR OLIVE OIL	2	HEADS LETTUCE
¼	C PLAIN OR GARLIC VINEGAR	2	AVOCADOS, PEELED AND SLICED
	JUICE OF 1 LEMON		CHOPPED CELERY TO TASTE
	SALT AND PEPPER TO TASTE		TOMATOES, PEELED AND QUARTERED

Add oil, vinegar, lemon juice, salt, and pepper to cheese. Beat with an electric mixer until creamy. Chop onions, including the green top of one, and mix in. Break lettuce into pieces. Add avocados, celery to taste, and tomatoes, if desired. Cover with dressing and toss, combining well. Serves 8.

CRAB LOUIS

4   LARGE LETTUCE
    LEAVES
4   HARD-BOILED EGGS,
    SLICED
1   C COOKED CRAB
    FLAKES
1   C SHREDDED
    LETTUCE
2   TBSP CHOPPED
    FRESH CHIVES

½   C UNSWEETENED
    FRENCH DRESSING
½   C CHILI SAUCE
1   TSP WORCESTERSHIRE
    SAUCE
2   HEAPING TBSP
    MAYONNAISE
    SALT AND PEPPER
      TO TASTE

Arrange lettuce leaves on four salad plates. Place one sliced egg on each leaf. Top with crabmeat, shredded lettuce, and chives that have been mixed together. Combine French dressing, chili sauce, Worcestershire sauce, mayonnaise, and seasonings. Beat well. Pour over crabmeat mounds. Serves 4.

S A L A D
D R E S S I N G S

2	EGG YOLKS		DASH OF TABASCO
2	C SALAD OIL		SAUCE
2	TBSP TARRAGON	1	HARD-BOILED EGG
	VINEGAR	1	SMALL GREEN BELL
	JUICE OF ½ LEMON		PEPPER, CHOPPED
¾	TSP SALT	2	PIMIENTOS
½	TSP SUGAR	¾	C CHILI SAUCE
⅛	TSP DRY MUSTARD	¼	C HEAVY CREAM,
			WHIPPED

B eat egg yolks well. In a separate bowl, combine vinegar, lemon juice, salt, sugar, mustard, and Tabasco sauce. Pour oil into beaten egg yolks very slowly while beating constantly, mixing in a little of the vinegar mixture between additions. Beat until very thick, adding more to thicken, if necessary.

Clean and chop egg, green pepper, and pimiento. Stir into mixture together with chili sauce. Chill. Just before serving blend in whipped cream. Serve on lettuce or shrimp cocktail. Makes about 4 cups.

OLIVE OIL SALAD DRESSING

½	TSP DRY MUSTARD	1	TSP MINCED ONION
½	TSP SALT	½	TSP MINCED PARSLEY
¼	TSP SUGAR	1	GARLIC CLOVE,
3	TBSP TARRAGON		CRUSHED
	VINEGAR	9	TBSP OLIVE OIL

Combine mustard, salt, and sugar. Mix in vinegar to make a smooth paste. Add onion, parsley, and crushed garlic. Let this stand for 1 hour. Remove garlic. Add olive oil gradually, stirring constantly. Pour over salad, using just enough dressing to coat each piece without leaving any surplus in the bottom of the bowl. Makes about ¾ cup.

CALIFORNIA DRESSING

1	C KETCHUP	1	TSP CELERY SALT
½	C HOT WATER	½	TSP ONION SALT
1	C SALAD OIL	½	C PREPARED
2	TBSP PREPARED		HORSERADISH
	MUSTARD	1	TBSP PAPRIKA
2	TBSP SUGAR	½	TBSP SALT

Mix all ingredients well. Cover and keep in the refrigerator. Makes 3 cups.

COUNTRY CLUB DRESSING

1	C MAYONNAISE	1	TSP PEPPER
1	TSP CHOPPED	1	GARLIC CLOVE,
	FRESH PARSLEY		MINCED
1	TSP CHOPPED		VINEGAR TO THIN
	FRESH CHIVES OR		
	SPRING ONION TOPS		

Mix all ingredients thoroughly and thin with vinegar until of desired consistency. Serve on a tossed green salad. Makes 1 cup.

FRUIT SALAD DRESSING

⅔ C SUGAR
2   TBSP FLOUR
2   EGGS, WELL BEATEN
1   C PINEAPPLE JUICE

JUICE OF 1 LEMON
JUICE OF 1 ORANGE
½   C WHIPPED CREAM

Combine sugar and flour. Add egg and fruit juices and mix until smooth. Cook over boiling water, stirring constantly, until thick. Cool. Fold in whipped cream. Serves 10.

ORANGE-MINT YOGURT DRESSING

1   C PLAIN LOW-FAT
    YOGURT
2   TBSP HONEY
2   TSP GRATED ORANGE
    PEEL
1½ TSP CANDIED
    GINGER, FINELY
    CHOPPED

⅛   TSP SALT
1   DASH CAYENNE
    PEPPER
1½ TSP CHOPPED FRESH
    MINT

Whisk together all ingredients until well combined.

OLD-FASHIONED COOKED SALAD DRESSING

¼   C SUGAR
¼   C FLOUR
½   TSP SALT
3   EGGS, SLIGHTLY
    BEATEN
½   C WATER

½   C VINEGAR
1   TSP PREPARED
    MUSTARD
1   6-OZ CAN
    EVAPORATED MILK,
    CHILLED

Combine sugar, flour, and salt. Mix in eggs, water, vinegar, and mustard. Cook over boiling water, stirring constantly, until thick. Chill. Add evaporated milk. Beat until light and fluffy and serve over shredded cabbage. Serves 6 to 8.

JADE GODDESS SALAD DRESSING

1	GARLIC CLOVE	2	TBSP CHOPPED FRESH CHIVES
3	C HOMEMADE MAYONNAISE	2	TSP CHOPPED FRESH PARSLEY
4	HEAPING TSP ANCHOVY PASTE		TARRAGON VINEGAR

Rub bowl with garlic. Put in mayonnaise, anchovy paste, chives, and parsley, and mix well. Thin slightly with vinegar. Makes about 4 cups.

MAYONNAISE

2	TBSP BUTTER, MELTED	½	TSP DRY MUSTARD
6	TBSP FLOUR	1	WHOLE EGG OR 2 EGG YOLKS
1	C HOT WATER	3	TBSP VINEGAR
1	TSP SALT	3	TBSP LEMON JUICE
1	TSP SUGAR	1	C SALAD OIL

Combine melted butter, flour, and hot water. Cook for 10 minutes, stirring constantly. Put salt, sugar, and mustard in a bowl and mix together well. Add egg, vinegar, lemon juice, and oil, but do not stir. Pour this into hot mixture and beat with a rotary beater until thick. Makes about 2½ cups.

GREEN GODDESS DRESSING

1	2-OZ CAN ANCHOVIES	⅓	C TARRAGON VINEGAR
1	LARGE AVOCADO, PEELED	⅓	C MAYONNAISE
1	GARLIC CLOVE, GRATED		

Drain anchovies, reserving oil. Put anchovies and avocado through a potato-ricer or food mill. Add garlic. Combine anchovy oil, vinegar, and mayonnaise. Add to avocado. Serve at once on shredded lettuce. Makes about 1¼ cups dressing.

VINAIGRETTE

1	GARLIC CLOVE	¼	TSP DRY MUSTARD
	SALT AND PEPPER	¼	C VINEGAR
	TO TASTE	⅔	C OLIVE OIL
1	TBSP LIGHT CORN		
	SYRUP OR SUGAR		

Rub a wooden bowl with garlic. Add salt and a generous amount of pepper. Add corn syrup and mustard. Work with a fork. Pour in vinegar and beat until dissolved. Slowly pour in olive oil. Mix well. Tear lettuce, add to dressing, and toss until well coated. Serve immediately. Makes a little less than 1 cup of dressing.

POPPY SEED DRESSING

½	C SUGAR	⅓	C VINEGAR
1	TSP DRY MUSTARD	⅓	MEDIUM ONION,
1	TSP SALT		GRATED
1	C OIL (SALAD AND	1⅓	TSP POPPY SEED
	OLIVE OIL)		

Mix together sugar, mustard, salt, oil, and vinegar. Beat with an electric mixer or with a rotary beater. Add onion and poppy seed last. This keeps indefinitely in the refrigerator. If it separates, beat again. Especially good on fruit salads. Makes about 1⅓ cups.

ROQUEFORT DRESSING

1	14-OZ BOTTLE KETCHUP	1	LARGE ONION, GRATED
	JUICE OF 2 LARGE GRAPEFRUIT	1	GARLIC CLOVE, MINCED
4	TBSP VINEGAR OR LEMON JUICE		SALT AND PEPPER TO TASTE
1½	TBSP SALAD OIL	½	LB ROQUEFORT CHEESE, GRATED

Combine all ingredients except cheese. Beat with a rotary egg beater until well mixed. Stir in cheese. Makes about 4 cups. Keeps indefinitely if stored in a glass jar in the refrigerator. Delicious on fruit salads.

SALAD DRESSING

1	TBSP SALT	¼	C GRATED PARMESAN CHEESE
1	TBSP DRY MUSTARD		
1	TSP SUGAR	5	TBSP MAYONNAISE
5	TBSP VINEGAR	1	GARLIC CLOVE
1	C OLIVE OIL		

Combine salt, mustard, sugar, and vinegar. Gradually add oil, cheese, and mayonnaise, beating constantly. Pour into jar with a clove of garlic. Chill. Shake well before using. Makes 2 cups.

SOUR CREAM DRESSING

1	WHOLE EGG OR 2	⅛	TSP PEPPER
	EGG YOLKS	½	TSP DRY MUSTARD
½	C SUGAR	¼	C VINEGAR
½	TSP SALT	¾	C SOUR CREAM

Beat egg (or egg yolks) well. Combine dry ingredients and gradually add to eggs while mixing. Blend in vinegar, then sour cream. Heat, stirring constantly, until mixture comes to a boil. Remove from fire, cool, and chill. Serve on salad greens, vegetable salad, or coleslaw. Makes 1½ cups.

FRENCH DRESSING

1	10½-OZ CAN	½	C SUGAR
	CONDENSED	2	TSP SALT
	TOMATO SOUP	¾	TSP DRY MUSTARD
1½	C SALAD OIL	3	TSP MINCED ONION
¾	C VINEGAR, SLIGHTLY		
	DILUTED		

Mix all ingredients well. Store in a covered jar in the refrigerator. Will keep 2 to 3 weeks.

SWEET FRENCH DRESSING

½	C VINEGAR	½	ONION, SLICED
9	TBSP SALAD OIL		SALT TO TASTE
½	C SUGAR		PAPRIKA TO COLOR

Combine all ingredients in a jar and shake well. Makes 2 cups.

BLUE CHEESE DRESSING

1½	LB GOOD DANISH BLUE CHEESE	¾	TBSP TABLESPOON LEMON JUICE
16	OZ BUTTERMILK*	3	QTS MAYONNAISE
9	TBSP WINE VINEGAR	2	TBSP ONION SALT
6	TBSP DRY SHERRY WINE	2	TBSP PEPPER
3	TBSP MINCED GARLIC	½	C PLUS 2 TBSP SOUR CREAM
¾	TSP TABASCO SAUCE		

Combine all ingredients. Age in refrigerator 24 hours. Pack in quart jars. Serves 20 or more. (If this is too much to use in two weeks, share with friends.)

* Use a good, acid, natural buttermilk or the dressing will not set.

HEAVENLY FRENCH DRESSING

½	C SALAD OIL	½	TSP SALT
3	TBSP VINEGAR	½	TSP WORCESTERSHIRE SAUCE
1	TBSP HORSERADISH DASH OF PEPPER	2	DASHES TABASCO SAUCE
1	GARLIC CLOVE, HALVED		

Combine all ingredients in a jar, cover, and chill. Shake well before using. Makes about ¾ cup of dressing.

S A U C E S

WILD WEST PICO DE GALLO

1½ C DICED RIPE
   TOMATOES
1 C CHOPPED SWEET
   ONION
1½ C DICED RIPE
   AVOCADO

2–3 TBSP FRESH LIME
   JUICE
¼ C CHOPPED FRESH
   CILANTRO
¼ TSP SALT
¼ TSP PEPPER

Combine all ingredients in small bowl. Refrigerate several hours for flavors to blend. Makes 4 cups. Spoon over fajitas, quesadillas, and grilled entrees or use as a dipping sauce for tortilla chips or sweet onion pieces.

TOMATO SAUCE

2 LB TOMATOES,
   CHOPPED
2 ONIONS, SLICED
   PARSLEY

   BAY LEAVES
2 PINCHES THYME
2 WHOLE CLOVES

Put tomatoes in enamel saucepan with onions, parsley, bay leaves, thyme, cloves, and wine. Simmer for 1 hour and press through a sieve.

116

HOLLANDAISE SAUCE

4	EGG YOLKS, SLIGHTLY BEATEN		FEW GRAINS PEPPER
2	TBSP VINEGAR	½	TSP CAYENNE PEPPER
½	TSP SALT		JUICE OF ½ LEMON
		½	C BUTTER, MELTED

Add vinegar, seasonings, and a few drops of lemon juice to egg yolks. Put in an earthenware bowl and place in a pan of hot water over the fire. Keep water hot, but never let it boil. Beat with a rotary beater until thick and fluffy. Gradually add lukewarm melted butter while beating. Stir in remaining lemon juice, and more salt if needed. If too thick, add a few drops of lukewarm water until the desired consistency is obtained. Serve immediately. This sauce may be made ahead of time and reheated, as long as it is at room temperature before reheating over hot water. Serves 6 to 8.

MUSHROOM SAUCE

½	LB MUSHROOMS	SALT AND PEPPER
3	TBSP BUTTER	TO TASTE
1	C HEAVY CREAM	
	FLOUR	

Wash mushrooms, scrubbing gently with a soft brush. Separate stems from caps. Sauté in butter in a heavy iron skillet until lightly browned. Pour in cream, bring to a boil, then turn fire as low as possible. Cook very slowly, stirring occasionally (mixture should hardly bubble).

Have some flour in a shaker. Two or three times during the cooking, sprinkle a little flour over the top of the sauce and stir in thoroughly. Use flour sparingly, as liquid will thicken as it cooks. Stir in salt and pepper. Cook for 20 to 25 minutes until mushrooms are tender. Serve with steak. Serves 4.

HOT BARBECUE SAUCE

2¼	TSP BUTTER, MELTED	3	TBSP PEPPER
3	C VINEGAR	1½	TSP CAYENNE
3	TBSP PREPARED		WORCESTERSHIRE
	MUSTARD		TO TASTE
3	TSP SALT		

Combine all ingredients well. Heat thoroughly. Use at once. This is a very hot sauce. Cayenne may be reduced, if desired. Makes about 3 cups.

RÉMOULADE SAUCE

4	HARD-BOILED EGGS, MINCED	2	STALKS CELERY, CHOPPED
1	TSP DRY MUSTARD	2	STUFFED OLIVES, MINCED
2	TBSP CHOPPED PARSLEY	1	C MAYONNAISE
¼	TSP MINCED GARLIC		SALT AND PEPPER
2	TBSP CHOPPED GREEN PEPPER		TO TASTE

Combine all ingredients and mix well. Serve with shrimp. Serves 4 to 6.

MUSTARD SAUCE

1	TBSP CORNSTARCH	3	EGGS, WELL BEATEN
2	TBSP SUGAR	½	C VINEGAR
3⅓	TBSP DRY MUSTARD	¼	C SALAD OIL

Combine cornstarch, sugar, and mustard. Mash with a spoon to remove any lumps. Mix in eggs and vinegar. Cook over boiling water, stirring constantly, until creamy. Remove from heat and beat in the salad oil with rotary beater. Makes about 1½ cups.

MUSTARD SAUCE FOR HAM

5   EGG YOLKS
5   TSP DRY MUSTARD
5   TSP SUGAR
1   SMALL JAR CURRANT
     JELLY

2   C VINEGAR
1   TSP CINNAMON
1   TSP ALLSPICE
1   TSP PAPRIKA
1   TSP SALT

Mix ingredients until very smooth. Cook in double boiler on medium fire until thick as cream. Serves 12.

MORNAY SAUCE

2   TBSP BUTTER
2   TBSP FLOUR
1   C MILK

1   C GRATED NEW YORK
     CHEESE
¼   C SHERRY
     SALT AND CAYENNE

In a skillet, melt butter and blend in flour. Add milk and cook, stirring until thickened. Mix in grated cheese until melted. Just before removing from the fire, add sherry, and seasonings to taste.

CREOLE SAUCE

2   TBSP BUTTER
¼   C CHOPPED ONION
6   GREEN OLIVES,
     CHOPPED
1   GARLIC CLOVE,
     MINCED
½   GREEN BELL PEPPER,
     CHOPPED
1½ C CANNED TOMATOES

PINCH THYME
1   SMALL BAY LEAF
1   TSP CHOPPED
     FRESH PARSLEY
⅓   TSP SALT
1   TSP SUGAR
     PINCH CAYENNE
     PEPPER

Melt butter over low heat. Add onion, olives, and garlic, and cook for 2 minutes. Add remaining ingredients and cook over medium heat until sauce is thick, about 45 minutes. Makes 2 cups.

HOT HORSERADISH SAUCE

2	TBSP BUTTER	3	TBSP WATER
2	TBSP FLOUR	1	TBSP VINEGAR
1	C MILK	½	TSP SALT
1	TBSP DEHYDRATED	½	TSP PAPRIKA
	HORSERADISH		

In a skillet, melt butter and blend in flour. Add milk and cook over a low flame, stirring constantly, until thickened. Soak horseradish in water for 10 minutes. Mix into cream sauce. Stir in vinegar, salt, and paprika. Cook for 2 to 3 minutes more. Serve hot with boiled beef, boiled tongue, roast beef, or pot roast. Serves 6.

SAUCE BÉARNAISE

3	TBSP TARRAGON VINEGAR	4	TBSP SOFTENED BUTTER
3	TBSP WATER	½	TSP SALT
½	ONION	½	TSP PAPRIKA
4	EGG YOLKS, SLIGHTLY BEATEN		

Combine vinegar, water, and onion in a saucepan and heat to the boiling point. Remove onion; pour mixture gradually into egg yolks, beating constantly. Place over boiling water and cook, stirring constantly, until slightly thickened. Add butter, 1 tablespoon at a time, stirring constantly. Cook until butter has melted and sauce has thickened. Season to taste with salt and paprika. Remove from heat at once and serve. This makes enough for 4 individual steaks.

SAUCE FOR WILD DUCK

2	TBSP BUTTER	½	C SHERRY
2	TBSP CURRANT JELLY		SALT AND PEPPER
	JUICE OF 1 LIME		CAYENNE PEPPER

Melt butter and jelly together over boiling water, blending well. Just before serving stir in lime juice, sherry, and seasonings to taste, and heat. Makes ¾ cup.

SAUCE FOR CHARCOAL-BROILED STEAKS

1	6-OZ BOTTLE A-1 SAUCE	3	GARLIC CLOVES, COARSELY CHOPPED
1	5-OZ BOTTLE WORCESTERSHIRE SAUCE	½	C BUTTER JUICE OF 1 LEMON

Combine all ingredients. Heat slowly until butter is melted. When broiling steaks or hamburgers over charcoal, brush generously with sauce after each turning. Makes about 2 cups.

SPICY COCKTAIL SAUCE

2	C SALAD OR OLIVE OIL		FEW DASHES TABASCO
½	C VINEGAR	1	ONION, GRATED
½	C LEMON JUICE	3	GARLIC CLOVES, MINCED
¼	14-OZ BOTTLE KETCHUP	1	TSP SALT
1	TBSP WORCESTERSHIRE SAUCE	1	TSP CAYENNE PEPPER
		1	TSP PAPRIKA
		1	6-OZ BOTTLE HORSERADISH

Combine all ingredients in the order given and mix well. Store in a covered jar in the refrigerator and use as needed on shrimp, crab meat, lobster, or oysters. Marinate seafood in sauce for 6 hours before serving. Makes 5 cups.

WHITE OR CREAM SAUCE (BÉCHAMEL)

2	TBSP BUTTER	2	WHOLE CLOVES	
1½	TBSP FLOUR		(OR SPRINKLE OF	
1	C MILK, SCALDED		GROUND CLOVES)	
1	SMALL ONION	½	SMALL BAY LEAF	

Melt butter over low heat. Add flour to make a roux and blend over low heat for 3 or 4 minutes. Remove roux from heat and let cool. When cool, stir in scalded milk (roux must be cool to avoid lumping). Add onion, cloves, and bay leaf. Cook over low heat, stirring with wire whisk or wooden spoon until thickened and very smooth. Place in 325°F oven for 25 minutes to cook slowly. Correct seasonings, remove bay leaf, and serve. For a richer sauce, substitute cream for milk. Makes 1 cup.

For variety of flavor, add one or more of the following just before serving: 1 teaspoon Worcestershire sauce; 1 teaspoon onion juice; 2 tablespoons chopped chives; a dash of nutmeg; 1 teaspoon lemon juice; 2 tablespoons chopped parsley; a dash of celery salt.

B R E A D S

FRESH CORN MUFFINS

4	EARS CORN, FRESH OR FROZEN (APPROXIMATELY 1½ C KERNELS)	2½	TSP BAKING POWDER
		½	TSP SALT

Grate corn off the cob. Add baking powder and salt and mix quickly. Fill well-greased muffin pan half full and bake in a 425°F oven for 25 minutes, or until a toothpick comes out clean. Serve hot with butter. Makes 6 to 8 muffins.

CHEESE STRAWS

1	LB SHARP CHEESE (WISCONSIN), GRATED		SALT AND CAYENNE PEPPER
1½	C FLOUR	¼	LB BUTTER
		1½	TSP BAKING FLOUR

Mix ingredients, roll out, and cut in strips, and bake at 375°F for 15 to 20 minutes.

SALT-RISING BREAD

2	WHITE POTATOES	2	C BOILING WATER
5	TBSP SUGAR	1	QT MILK
2	TBSP WHITE		FLOUR
	CORNMEAL	2	TBSP SALT
	PINCH OF BAKING		SHORTENING
	SODA		

At noon before you make bread, slice two medium-size Irish potatoes into a quart jar. Add 2 tablespoons sugar, white cornmeal, and a small pinch of baking soda. Pour boiling water into the jar. Put on the lid but do not screw it down. Set in a warm place until morning, when the mixture should have about an inch of foam at the top and an odd odor. If it doesn't, do not use it. The success of salt-rising bread depends on the yeast. Thus, you are saved much time and ingredients by getting the yeast just right.

Scald, but do not boil, the sweet milk; cool to lukewarm; add 2 tablespoons of sugar, a small pinch of baking soda, and one cup of the liquid drained from the jar containing the yeast. Add enough flour to make a stiff batter. Set in a warm place until it doubles in bulk. Add salt, shortening about the size of an egg, and 1 tablespoon of sugar. Add enough flour to make dough stiff enough to handle. Knead 20 minutes, make into loaves, put into greased pans, and let rise in a warm place until it doubles in bulk. Bake in 350°F oven for one hour.

WAFFLES

1¾	C FLOUR	3	EGGS, SEPARATED
2	TSP BAKING POWDER	1½	C MILK
2	TSP SUGAR	6	TBSP MELTED BUTTER
1	TSP SALT		BUTTER AND SYRUP

Sift together flour, baking powder, sugar, and salt. Beat egg yolks well and add milk and butter. Combine sifted and liquid ingredients. Beat egg whites stiff and fold into batter. Grease a hot waffle iron and pour in batter. Bake 4 to 5 minutes. Serve hot with butter and syrup.

DOWN HOME YEAST ROLLS

2	PACKAGES YEAST	1	C SUGAR
2	C WARM WATER	1	TSP SALT
1	LARGE TBSP SHORTENING, MELTED	5½	C FLOUR

Dissolve yeast in warm—not hot—water. Mix all ingredients together, stirring in the flour a little at a time. Cover and let rise. Roll out and cut with biscuit cutter. Roll gently in more melted shortening (to keep from cracking). Bake in 400°F oven 10 to 12 minutes until golden brown.

APPLE CHEDDAR PECAN BREAD

3	C BISCUIT MIX	2	C CHOPPED, PEELED APPLES
¼	C SUGAR	¾	C CHOPPED PECANS
½	TSP GROUND CINNAMON	1	C (4 OZ) SHREDDED SHARP NATURAL CHEDDAR CHEESE
1	EGG		
½	C MILK		

Combine biscuit mix, sugar, cinnamon, egg, and milk. Stir vigorously for 30 seconds. Stir in apples, pecans, and cheese. Pour into 9 x 5 x 3 greased loaf pan. Bake at 350°F for 55 to 60 minutes. Cool before slicing. Makes 1 loaf.

DOWN HOME DUTCH OVEN CORNBREAD

¾	C FLOUR		¼	C SUGAR
1½	C YELLOW CORNMEAL		2	TBSP SHORTENING
			¾	C MILK
1	HEAPING TBSP BAKING POWDER		1	EGG
½	TSP SALT		4	TBSP BACON GREASE

Mix dry ingredients well (mix the hound out of it). Add shortening. Cut like pie dough. Add enough milk mixed with one whole egg to make batter a little thinner than pancake batter.

Put bacon grease in bottom of pan. Make sure it covers bottom. Heat grease and then pour mixture into heated Dutch oven. Bake, uncovered, in 425°F oven approximately 20 minutes or until golden brown.

TEXAS HOE CAKES

1	C WHITE CORN MEAL	1–2	TBSP BACON FAT OR BUTTER
¾	C BOILING WATER		
½	TSP (PINCH) OF SALT		

Combine cornmeal and salt in bowl. Stirring mixture constantly, add boiling water in slow, thin stream. Beat until batter is smooth. Pat out hoe cakes (if mixture is too hot flatten with spoon). Place on cast iron griddle or skillet coated with bacon fat or butter and fry until golden brown. Turn over and repeat. *Do not deep fry.*

Hoe cakes are excellent with red beans, fresh sliced onions, and beef brisket.

BANANA-NUT BREAD

1	C MASHED RIPE BANANAS	1	EGG
⅓	C LOW-FAT (1%) BUTTERMILK	2	CUPS SIFTED FLOUR
		1	TSP BAKING POWDER
½	C PACKED BROWN SUGAR	½	TSP BAKING SODA
		½	TSP SALT
¼	C MARGARINE	½	C CHOPPED PECANS

Preheat oven to 350°F. Lightly oil 9 x 5 x 3 inch pan. Stir together mashed bananas and buttermilk; set aside. Cream brown sugar and margarine together until light. Beat in egg. Add banana mixture; beat well. Sift together flour, baking powder, baking soda and salt; add all at once to liquid ingredients. Stir until well blended. Stir in nuts and turn into pan. Bake for 50 to 55 minutes or until toothpick inserted in center comes out clean. Cool 5 minutes in pan. Remove from pan and complete cooling on a wire rack before slicing. Makes one loaf (18, ½-inch slices).

SPICED PUMPKIN BREAD

3	C SUGAR	1	TSP GROUND NUTMEG
1	C VEGETABLE OIL		
3	LARGE EGGS	1	TSP BAKING SODA
1	16-OZ CAN SOLID PACKED PUMPKIN	½	TSP SALT
		½	TSP BAKING POWDER
3	C FLOUR	1	C CHOPPED WALNUTS (OPTIONAL)
1	TSP GROUND CLOVES		
1	TSP GROUND CINNAMON		

Preheat oven to 350°F. Butter and flour two 9 x 5 x 3 inch loaf pans. Beat sugar and oil in large bowl. Mix in eggs and pumpkin. Sift flour, cloves, cinnamon, nutmeg, baking soda, salt, and baking powder into another bowl. Stir into pumpkin mixture in 2 additions. Mix in walnuts. Divide batter equally into pans. Bake until tester comes out clean (about 1 hour and 10 minutes). Transfer to racks and cool 10 minutes. Using a sharp knife, cut around edge of loaves and turn out onto racks to cool completely. Makes 2 loaves.

KUCHEN (GERMAN COFFEE CAKE)

2	C MILK	3	EGGS, BEATEN
1	C WATER	8–9	C FLOUR
1	TBSP SALT	2	C RAISINS
1	C SUGAR		GROUND CINNAMON
½	C MARGARINE,		(FOR SPRINKLING
	MELTED		JUST BEFORE
2	PKGS YEAST		BAKING)
¼	C WARM WATER		

Scald milk and cool by adding the water. Add salt, sugar, and melted margarine. Add yeast which has been dissolved in ¼ cup warm water. Add beaten eggs. Add about 4 cups of flour and beat. Add raisins and then add additional flour 1 cup at a time, beating after each addition, until dough can be handled. Knead until elastic. Put in greased bowl, cover, and let rise until double in size. Punch down and knead again. Form into round, walnut-sized balls and place in shallow pans (such as round layer cake pans). Let rise about 30 minutes or until almost double. Preheat oven to 350°F. Moisten tops of loaves with water; sprinkle with cinnamon and bake about 30 to 40 minutes or until tops are golden brown.

D E S S E R T S

VANILLA ICEBOX CAKE

2	C POWDERED SUGAR	2	TSP VANILLA	
1	TSP COCOA	2	EGG WHITES, STIFFLY	
¼	TSP SALT		BEATEN	
½	C BUTTER	1½	C VANILLA WAFER	
2	EGG YOLKS		CRUMBS	
1	C CHOPPED TOASTED, SALTED PECANS			

Sift sugar, cocoa, and salt together. Cream butter, add mixture of sugar gradually, and blend until very light. Add egg yolks, one at a time, beating well after each addition. Mix in chopped nuts and vanilla. Fold in egg whites.

Place part of the wafer crumbs on the bottom of the pan. Pour in filling and top with remaining crumbs. Chill in the refrigerator for at least 2 hours. Serves 8 to 10.

CRANBERRY FRAPPÉ

1	QT FRESH CRANBERRIES	2	C SUGAR JUICE OF 2 LEMONS
2	C WATER	1	PT WHIPPED CREAM

To the quart of cranberries add water and boil until they burst open. Strain, then add sugar and juice of 2 lemons. Let cool. Add whipped cream and freeze. Serve in compote glasses. Excellent with turkey.

PORCUPINE PUDDING

1	C BUTTER	1	TSP VANILLA
2	C POWDERED SUGAR	18	LADYFINGERS
½	C STRONG COFFEE	2	C BLANCHED
6	EGG YOLKS, WELL BEATEN		ALMONDS
		1	PT WHIPPED CREAM

Cream butter, add sugar gradually, and beat until smooth. Blend in coffee, egg yolks, and vanilla. Line a ring mold with split ladyfingers. Pour in coffee mixture. Chill in the refrigerator for 12 hours or more.

Split almonds, invert pudding on a serving plate, and remove mold. Stick almonds into it to resemble a porcupine. Fill center with sweetened whipped cream. Serves 8.

SCHAUM TORTE

6	EGG WHITES	STRAWBERRIES OR
2	C SUGAR	COCONUT
1	TSP VANILLA	WHIPPED CREAM
2	TBSP VINEGAR	

Beat egg whites stiff. While beating constantly, gradually add sugar, vanilla, and vinegar. Pour into greased springform pan with hole in center. Bake in slow oven 1 hour. Cool and fill with fresh strawberries or coconut and whipped cream.

PINEAPPLE UPSIDE-DOWN CAKE

2	EGG YOLKS, WELL BEATEN	2	EGG WHITES, STIFFLY BEATEN
1	C SUGAR	½	C BUTTER
6	TBSP HOT MILK	1	C BROWN SUGAR
1	GENEROUS C SIFTED FLOUR	5	SLICES PINEAPPLE
1	TSP VANILLA	¼	C CHOPPED PECANS

Gradually add ½ cup of sugar and the milk to the egg yolks. Beat well. Mix in the remaining ½ cup sugar, flour, and vanilla thoroughly. Fold in egg whites.

Melt butter in a large cast-iron skillet. Add brown sugar and blend well. Over this arrange pineapple and nuts in a symmetrical pattern. Cover with batter. Bake at 350°F 25 to 30 minutes, or until done. Invert immediately onto a serving dish.

BANANA PUDDING

¾	C SUGAR	2	C MILK
⅓	C FLOUR	½	TSP VANILLA EXTRACT
	DASH SALT	35–40	VANILLA WAFERS
4	EGGS, SEPARATED (AT ROOM TEMPERATURE)	3–4	BANANAS, SLICED

Combine ½ cup sugar, flour, and salt in top of double boiler. Stir in 4 egg yolks and milk; blend well. Cook uncovered over boiling water. Stir constantly until thickened. Reduce heat and cook, stirring constantly, for 5 minutes. Remove from heat; add vanilla. Spread small amount of custard on bottom of 1½-quart casserole; cover with layer of vanilla wafers. Top with layers of sliced bananas; pour ⅓ of custard over bananas. Continue to layer wafers, bananas, and custard to make 3 layers of each, ending with custard. Beat egg whites until stiff but not dry. Gradually add remaining ¼ cup of sugar and beat until stiff peaks form. Spoon on top of pudding, spreading to edges. Bake at 425°F for 5 minutes or until delicately brown. Cool slightly or chill. Serves 4 to 6.

BLUEBERRY TORTILLA PIZZA

½ C RICOTTA CHEESE
1 TBSP POWDERED
    SUGAR
1 PT FRESH
    BLUEBERRIES
½ C SLICED
    STRAWBERRIES
1 LARGE (10-INCH)
    FLOUR TORTILLA

1 TBSP BUTTER,
    MELTED
2 TSP CINNAMON
    SUGAR
¼ C TOASTED
    SHREDDED
    COCONUT*

Preheat broiler. In a small bowl, combine ricotta cheese and confectioners' sugar; set aside. In another bowl, combine blueberries and strawberries. Arrange tortilla on a broiler pan; brush with butter and sprinkle with cinnamon sugar. Broil about 6 inches from heat source, until lightly browned, about 3 minutes. Cool slightly. Spread ricotta mixture on the tortilla; top with blueberry mixture and then sprinkle with coconut. Serves 4.

*To toast coconut, place in a skillet over moderate heat until pale gold, stirring constantly.

APPLE-RAISIN BREAD PUDDING

3 C DAY-OLD BREAD
    CUBES (6–7 SLICES)
1 APPLE, THINLY SLICED
½ C RAISINS
3 EGGS, SLIGHTLY
    BEATEN

⅓ C SUGAR
    DASH OF SALT
½ TSP VANILLA EXTRACT
2 C SCALDED MILK
    GROUND CINNAMON

In greased 1-quart casserole, place alternate layers of bread cubes, apple slices, and raisins. In a large bowl, combine eggs, sugar, salt, and vanilla. Gradually blend in the scalded milk. Pour over bread cubes. Sprinkle cinnamon over top of pudding before placing in oven. Set uncovered casserole in a pan of hot water (about ½ inch of water) and bake at 325°F for 1 hour or until a knife inserted halfway between center and outside edges comes out clean. Serves 6.

UPSIDE-DOWN LEMON CUPS

1	C SUGAR	1	TBSP BUTTER, MELTED
3	TBSP SIFTED FLOUR	2	EGG YOLKS, SLIGHTLY BEATEN
	PINCH OF SALT	1	C MILK
	JUICE AND GRATED RIND OF 1 LARGE LEMON	2	EGG WHITES, STIFFLY BEATEN

Combine sugar, flour, salt, lemon juice and rind, melted butter, egg yolks, and milk. Fold in egg whites. Place in greased custard cups and set in a pan of hot water. Bake at 350°F 30 to 35 minutes. Cool and chill.

Remove from cups to serve, turning upside down. This is a complete dessert in itself, or may be used on ice cream or other desserts. Serves 6.

ENGLISH TOFFEE ICEBOX PIE

½	C BUTTER	3	TBSP BRANDY
½	C GRANULATED SUGAR	1	TSP VANILLA
2	C POWDERED SUGAR	1	C CHOPPED SALTED, TOASTED PECANS
¼	TSP SALT	2	EGG WHITES, STIFFLY BEATEN
1	TSP COCOA	1½	C VANILLA WAFER CRUMBS
2	EGG YOLKS		

Cream butter. Gradually blend in granulated sugar. Combine powdered sugar, cocoa, and salt and add slowly to butter mixture, mixing thoroughly. Beat in egg yolks well. Add brandy, vanilla, and pecans. Fold in egg whites.

Line an 8 x 10 pan with waxed paper. Spread about three-quarters of the crumbs on bottom of the pan. Pour in filling and sprinkle with remaining crumbs. Chill in the refrigerator for at least 2 hours. Serves 6.

CHOCOLATE-MARSHMALLOW ICEBOX CAKE

½ C BUTTER
½ C POWDERED SUGAR
3 EGG YOLKS, WELL
  BEATEN
⅔ C CHOCOLATE SYRUP
16 MARSHMALLOWS,
  QUARTERED
  PECANS, AS DESIRED

1 C HEAVY CREAM,
  WHIPPED
3 EGG WHITES,
  STIFFLY BEATEN
16 GRAHAM CRACKERS

ream butter, add sugar gradually, and mix until very light. Beat in egg yolks and chocolate syrup well. Add marshmallows and pecans. Fold in whipped cream, then egg whites. Roll graham crackers into fine crumbs. Put half in the bottom of a casserole and pour in half the chocolate mixture. Top with the remaining crumbs and filling. Chill for 24 hours. Serve with additional whipped cream. Serves 8.

APPLE BROWN BETTY

4 C THINLY SLICED,
  PEELED APPLES
2 C BREAD CUBES OR
  TORN BREAD PIECES
½ C FIRMLY PACKED
  BROWN SUGAR

⅛ TSP GROUND
  CINNAMON
2 TBSP MARGARINE
¼ C HOT WATER

rease 1-quart baking dish. Arrange half of apples on bottom of dish. Follow with half of bread, then half of sugar. Repeat layers. Sprinkle cinnamon over top. Cut margarine in pieces and lay them on top. Finish by pouring hot water over all. Cover and bake at 350°F for 30 minutes; uncover and bake 10 minutes longer. Serve warm or chilled. Serves 4.

Apple Cheese Betty: Spoon 1 cup ricotta cheese over first layer of apples, bread, and sugar. Complete as above.

COCONUT DELIGHT

2	LARGE RIPE COCONUTS (TO MAKE 2 C OF DILUTED COCONUT MILK)	6	EGG YOLKS
		16	LADYFINGERS
		3	EGG WHITES
3⅓	C SUGAR	3	TBSP SUGAR

In saucepan, combine coconut milk and sugar and cook over high heat without stirring until it boils. Reduce heat to moderate and boil until syrup thickens to a light stage (candy thermometer reads 220°F). Remove from heat and allow to cool. Place egg yolks in a saucepan and blend in the syrup gradually. Cook over moderate heat, stirring constantly with a wooden spoon, until it boils. Remove immediately from heat and strain. For each serving, place 2 ladyfingers in deep dessert plates and spoon coconut cream over them. Beat egg whites until stiff, add sugar gradually, and beat. Garnish dessert with the meringue. Serves 8.

FLOATING ISLANDS

2	C MILK	1	TSP FLOUR
4	EGG WHITES	1	TSP VANILLA OR ALMOND EXTRACT
4	EGG YOLKS		
½	C SUGAR		

Scald milk in top of double boiler, beat egg whites until stiff, and add ¼ cup of the sugar gradually. Drop several spoonfuls of egg white mixture into the hot milk, cover, and cook 4 minutes. Remove puffs carefully with a perforated spoon and drain. Drop additional spoonfuls into hot milk until all puffs are cooked. Beat egg yolks lightly, add remaining ¼ cup of the sugar and the flour, stir into milk, and continue stirring until mixture thickens. Flavor with vanilla or almond extract. Chill the custard; then top with puffs.

PEACH TART

CRUST

1¼	C FLOUR	1	EGG YOLK
¼	TSP SALT	1½	TBSP OR MORE COLD
3	TBSP SUGAR		WATER
10	TBSP UNSALTED		
	BUTTER, CHILLED		

Place flour, salt, and sugar in work bowl of a food processor. Cut butter into tablespoon-sized pieces and add them. Process, using rapid off-on pulses, until mixture resembles small particles about the size of oatmeal flakes. In small bowl, stir together egg yolk and 1½ tablespoons water. With processor running, pour egg mixture into bowl. Dump dough onto a work surface and gather into a ball. Press and pat walnut-sized pieces of dough over the bottom and sides of a tart pan with removable bottom, leaving no gaps and making it as even as you can. Bake at 425º F for 8 to 10 minutes or until light golden brown. Cool completely.

FILLING

1	C CHILLED	6	LARGE PEACHES,
	MASCARPONE		PITTED, PEELED
½	C POWDERED SUGAR		IF DESIRED,
1	TSP GRATED		AND SLICED
	ORANGE ZEST		¼-INCH THICK
1	TSP VANILLA EXTRACT	¼	C APRICOT JAM,
½	C CHILLED HEAVY		WARMED UNTIL
	CREAM		LIQUEFIED

In medium bowl, mix mascarpone and powdered sugar and stir until smooth. Add orange zest and vanilla extract. Whip cream until soft peaks form and fold into the mascarpone mixture. Spread mixture into baked and cooled tart crust. Top with peach slices. Brush peaches with the liquefied apricot jam to glaze. Refrigerate tart at least one hour or overnight before serving. Serves 6 to 8.

DOWN HOME APPLE CRISP

10–12	WINESAP APPLES	2	C FLOUR
5	TBSP CINNAMON	1¾	C FIRMLY PACKED
2	TBSP WATER		LIGHT BROWN SUGAR
2	STICKS BUTTER, CUT		
	INTO PIECES		

C over sides and bottom of Dutch oven with butter. Peel and slice apples. Place apples in Dutch oven; sprinkle with water and 3 tablespoons of cinnamon. Fold in butter and remaining cinnamon and slowly add flour. Add light brown sugar. Pack on top of apples. Cover with Dutch oven lid. Bake in oven at 350°F for 30 minutes or until topping is brown.

HOT FRUIT COMPOTE

½	C CHOPPED PRUNES	1	TSP CINNAMON
½	C CHOPPED PEARS	½	TSP GINGER
½	C CHOPPED PEACHES	½	TSP NUTMEG
½	C CHOPPED		JUICE AND GRATED
	PINEAPPLE		RIND OF ½ LEMON
1½	C APPLESAUCE		

C ombine prunes, pears, peaches, and pineapple with applesauce and arrange in ovenproof casserole dish. Then add cinnamon, ginger, and nutmeg. Add the lemon juice and rind. Mix the fruits, cover, and place in a slow 250°F oven for at least 1 hour before serving. The longer it bakes, the better it is. Other fruits can be substituted, and either fresh or canned fruits may be used. This makes a delicious condiment with all meat and fowl. Serve hot.

BLUEBERRY BUCKLE

2	C SIFTED FLOUR	1	EGG
2	TSP BAKING POWDER	½	C MILK
½	TSP SALT	2	C FRESH OR FROZEN
¼	C SOFT BUTTER		BLUEBERRIES
1	C SUGAR		

Sift together flour, baking powder, and salt. Cream butter and sugar until light and fluffy. Add egg and milk and beat well. Add flour, baking powder, and salt and stir until blended. Add blueberries. Spread mixture into 9 x 13 inch pan.

TOPPING

¼	C SOFT BUTTER	⅓	C FLOUR
½	C PACKED BROWN	½	TSP GROUND
	SUGAR		CINNAMON

Cream together butter and sugar. Combine flour and cinnamon and add to creamed mixture. Stir until crumbly. Sprinkle over blueberry buckle and bake 35 to 45 minutes at 350°F. Serves 6.

BAKED FUDGE

8	EGGS, BEATEN	2	C MARGARINE OR
4	C SUGAR		BUTTER, MELTED
1	C FLOUR	2	C CHOPPED PECANS
1	C COCOA	3½	TSP VANILLA EXTRACT
		½	TSP SALT

Beat eggs until lemon colored. Add sugar, flour, and cocoa and mix until well blended. Add melted butter or margarine. Stir in remaining ingredients and pour into a 15 x 10 inch pan. Set pan in larger pan of water. Bake at 325°F for 45 to 50 minutes or until set like custard. Serve warm with whipped cream or ice cream. Serves 20.

APPLE DUMPLINGS

1	BASIC PIE CRUST RECIPE	¼	C BUTTER
8	GRANNY SMITH APPLES	½	C BROWN SUGAR
½	C RAISINS	½	C MAPLE SYRUP
		½	C WATER

Divide dough into eight equal portions. Roll each into a circle of approximately the same thickness. Peel apples; slice vertically in half and core. Place a tablespoon of raisins, a dab of butter, and a teaspoon of brown sugar in the center of one apple half; layer another half on top to form a whole apple. Repeat with remaining apples. Wrap each apple in dough and place in a glass 9 x 12 inch pan. Combine syrup, water, remaining butter, and brown sugar in a saucepan. Heat and pour over the apples. Bake at 400°F for 1 hour or until pastry is golden and apples are tender. Serve with the sauce from the dish. Serves 8.

DOWN HOME RICE PUDDING

1½	C COOKED RICE	3	EGGS
½	C RAISINS	1	TSP VANILLA FLAVORING
½	C SUGAR		CINNAMON FOR SPRINKLING
2	C MILK		

Mix first six ingredients well. Pour into ovenproof casserole dish. Sprinkle cinnamon on top. Bake, uncovered, at 325°F for 25 minutes. Rich and delicious.

D E S S E R T
S A U C E S

CHOCOLATE SAUCE I

8	SQ UNSWEETENED CHOCOLATE	2	TBSP BUTTER
			PINCH OF SALT
4	EGG YOLKS	3	C SUGAR
1	C MILK	½	TBSP VANILLA

Melt chocolate in double boiler. Combine all other ingredients except vanilla and beat constantly until it comes to a boil. Cook 1 minute, then add chocolate and vanilla.

CHOCOLATE SAUCE II

3	SQ UNSWEETENED CHOCOLATE	1	C SUGAR
	PINCH OF SALT	1½	C SOUR CREAM

Melt chocolate in a heavy pan over a low flame. Mix in sugar, sour cream, and salt. Simmer, without stirring, until mixture boils. Continue to cook, stirring occasionally, for 10 minutes. Serve warm. Makes 2 cups.

DESSERT SAUCE

¼	C BUTTER	JUICE AND GRATED
¼	C POWDERED SUGAR	RIND OF 1 LEMON
1	TBSP MILK	JUICE AND GRATED
		RIND OF 1 ORANGE

Cream butter, add sugar gradually, and beat until very light. Mix in milk. Place over boiling water and cook, while stirring, for 3 or 4 minutes, until mixture is the consistency of thick cream.

Remove from the heat. Add juice and rind of lemon or orange or both. Serve over gingerbread or puddings. Serves 4 to 6.

HARD SAUCE

1	C BUTTER	1	EGG WHITE, OR
1½	C POWDERED SUGAR	2	TBSP HEAVY CREAM
			WHISKEY OR SHERRY

Cream butter, add sugar gradually, and mix until smooth. Add egg white or cream and beat well. Gradually blend in whiskey or sherry to taste. Serves 8 to 10.

LEMON SAUCE

½	C BUTTER	GRATED RIND OF
1	C SUGAR	1 LEMON
1	EGG, WELL BEATEN	JUICE OF 2–3 LEMONS
1	TSP NUTMEG	3	TBSP HOT WATER

Cream butter and sugar together in a saucepan. Mix in egg, nutmeg, lemon rind, and juice. Add hot water. Cook over a very low flame, stirring constantly, 15 to 20 minutes or until thick. Serves 6.

MOCK DEVONSHIRE CREAM

1	3-OZ PKG CREAM CHEESE	1	TBSP LEMON JUICE
¼	TSP GRATED LEMON RIND	1½	TSP SUGAR
		⅓	C CREAM

Mash the cream cheese with a fork. Blend in the remaining ingredients. It should be the consistency of a very heavy cream. If a thinner sauce is desired, add a little canned-fruit syrup. Serve over apricots, peaches, or other fruit. Makes 4 servings.

RUM SAUCE

1	C BROWN SUGAR	½	TSP GRATED LEMON RIND
½	C WATER		
1	TBSP BUTTER	1	TSP LEMON JUICE
		2	TBSP RUM

Combine brown sugar, water, and butter. Cook for about 15 minutes, or until it forms a syrup. Stir in lemon rind, lemon juice, and rum. Serve hot over cake. Makes about 6 servings.

BUTTER SAUCE FOR CAKE

1	C SUGAR	1	EGG, WELL BEATEN
¼	C BUTTER	½	TSP LEMON EXTRACT
½	C WATER	½	TSP VANILLA

Combine sugar, butter, and water and bring to a boil. Pour very slowly into egg, beating constantly. Mix in lemon extract and vanilla. Serve immediately, over cake or gingerbread. Makes 6 servings.

CHEWY CHOCOLATE SAUCE

1 SQ UNSWEETENED CHOCOLATE	1 C SUGAR
1 TBSP BUTTER	3 TBSP BOILING WATER
¼ C LIGHT CORN SYRUP	1 TSP VANILLA

Melt chocolate and butter in top of a double boiler. Add corn syrup, sugar, and boiling water. Cook over direct heat for 3 to 10 minutes. Test sauce, as it cooks, on a little ice cream. When it hardens over the ice cream, it should be done. If it gets too chewy, add a little more water and bring to a boil again. Add vanilla and serve warm. Serves 2 to 3.

I C E S A N D
I C E C R E A M

STRAWBERRY SHERBET

2 C SUGAR
2 C WATER
2 QTS STRAWBERRIES
JUICE OF 1 LEMON

JUICE OF 2–3
ORANGES
1 C HEAVY CREAM,
WHIPPED

Combine sugar and water in a saucepan and bring to a boil. Cook for about 3 minutes, or until a syrup is formed. Cool. Wash, hull, and mash strawberries. Mix into syrup together with lemon and orange juice. Freeze in a refrigerator tray until mushy. Stir well and fold in whipped cream. Continue to freeze until hard. Top individual servings with additional whipped cream and whole strawberries. Serves 12 to 14.

ORANGE SHERBET

2 C SUGAR
2 C WATER

4 C ORANGE JUICE
JUICE OF 1 LEMON

Combine sugar and water. Bring to a boil and cook for 10 minutes. Stir in orange and lemon juice. Freeze in a refrigerator tray for at least 6 hours, stirring four or five times. Makes 2 trays.

PEACH ICE CREAM

1½	C SUGAR	3	DROPS ALMOND
1	QT HEAVY CREAM		EXTRACT
1	QT MILK	12	MEDIUM-SIZE
3	DROPS LEMON		OVERRIPE PEACHES
	EXTRACT		

Combine sugar, cream, milk, and extracts. Freeze in an ice cream freezer. When about half frozen, mix in peaches that have been peeled and mashed well. Continue to freeze until hard. Makes 1 gallon.

PEACH ICE CREAM

10–12	RIPE PEACHES, PEELED	¾	C SUGAR
	AND SLICED	1	TSP VANILLA
1	SMALL PKG VANILLA		FLAVORING
	INSTANT PUDDING		MILK
1	CAN SWEETENED		(APPROXIMATELY
	CONDENSED MILK		½ GAL)

In large bowl, chop peaches into small bits. Add vanilla pudding, sweetened condensed milk, sugar, and vanilla flavoring. Stir well. Pour into ice cream freezer. Add milk to "full" line and freeze until hard.

QUICK LEMON ICE CREAM

1	C SUGAR	2	TSP GRATED LEMON
3	TBSP LEMON JUICE		RIND
		1	PT HEAVY CREAM

Mix sugar, lemon juice, and rind. Gradually beat in cream. Pour into freezer ice cube tray and freeze 3 hours without stirring. Serves 4.

THREE-FRUIT SHERBET

1½	C SUGAR	JUICE OF 3 ORANGES
3	C WATER	JUICE OF 3 LEMONS
3	BANANAS	1 EGG WHITE, STIFFLY
	GRATED RIND OF	BEATEN
	1 ORANGE	

Combine sugar and water. Bring to a boil and cook for 5 minutes or until a syrup is formed. Cool.

Press bananas through a sieve and add to syrup. Mix in orange rind and juices. Place in a refrigerator tray and freeze until mushy. Fold in egg white thoroughly. Continue to freeze until hard. Makes 1 quart.

VANILLA ICE CREAM

1½	C SUGAR	¼	TSP SALT
¼	C PLUS 2 TBSP FLOUR	1½	C COFFEE CREAM
3	EGGS, SLIGHTLY	1½	TSP VANILLA
	BEATEN	3	C HEAVY CREAM

Combine sugar and flour. Add salt and coffee cream to eggs, and mix gradually into the dry ingredients. Beat until smooth. Cook over boiling water, stirring constantly, until it forms a thick custard. Strain and cool. Add vanilla and heavy cream. Chill. Freeze in ice cream freezer. Makes about 2 quarts.

PEPPERMINT ICE CREAM

¾	LB PEPPERMINT	1	C HEAVY CREAM,
	CANDY		WHIPPED
1	C COFFEE CREAM		

Place candy in a cloth sack and mash well. Add to coffee cream and heat over boiling water until peppermint is melted. Cool. Fold in whipped cream. Freeze in an ice cream freezer. Serves 4.

CANTALOUPE ICE

4½	C WATER	¾	C LEMON JUICE
2½	C SUGAR	2	EGG WHITES
9	C CANTALOUPE PULP AND JUICE		BLACK CHERRIES

Boil water and sugar together for 5 minutes. Add cantaloupe pulp and juice, lemon juice, and egg whites. Freeze. Serve in large dish with black cherries (fresh, if possible) that have been soaked in brandy. Serves 14.

PLUM BERRY ICE CREAM

3	TBSP CORNSTARCH	1	C PUREED FRESH PLUMS
1	12-OZ CAN EVAPORATED WHOLE MILK	1	C PUREED FRESH OR FROZEN BERRIES (STRAWBERRIES, RASPBERRIES, OR BLUEBERRIES)
¼	C SUGAR		
1	ENVELOPE UNFLAVORED GELATIN	1	C NONFAT DRY MILK POWDER
¼	C WATER		

Cook cornstarch, evaporated milk, and sugar over medium-high heat until thickened. Cool. Soften gelatin in water, heating over low heat to dissolve. Place cooled custard, gelatin, plum puree, berries, and dry milk in food processor or blender. Mix until blended. Freeze in ice cream maker according to manufacturer's directions. Serve at once or pack into freezer containers. Makes 8 servings.

HOMEMADE STRAWBERRY ICE CREAM

1	5½-OZ PKG VANILLA INSTANT PUDDING MIX	1	13-OZ CAN EVAPORATED MILK
2	C SUGAR	2	C MASHED FRESH STRAWBERRIES
5	C MILK		

Combine pudding mix and sugar in a large bowl. Add milk and evaporated milk, stirring well until sugar is dissolved. Add mashed strawberries to mixture. Pour mixture into freezer can and set in refrigerator for 2 hours to chill. Freeze according to manufacturer's instructions. Let set in freezer for 1 hour before serving. Makes 1 gallon.

P I E ★ S

KENTUCKY CHESS PIE

3	EGG YOLKS	5	TBSP MILK
1	EGG WHITE	½	TSP VANILLA
1	C SUGAR	1	8-INCH PIE SHELL,
2	TBSP FLOUR		UNBAKED
½	C BUTTER, MELTED		MERINGUE

Beat egg yolks and egg white together. Combine sugar and flour, and add to eggs along with melted butter, milk, and vanilla. Pour into an unbaked 8-inch shell and cook at 400°F 30 to 35 minutes. When filling is set and pie is done, cover with a meringue and bake at 300°F to brown lightly.

PECAN PIE

3	EGGS	1	8-INCH UNBAKED
½	C SUGAR		PIE SHELL
3	TBSP FLOUR	1	C PECAN HALVES
1½	C DARK CORN SYRUP		

Add sugar to eggs and beat until very thick. Mix in flour, then corn syrup. Pour into pie shell and top with pecans. Bake at 300°F for 45 minutes, or until firm. Serves 6.

EGG NOG PIE

1¼	C MILK	5	TBSP BRANDY OR RUM
1	C SUGAR	2	EGG WHITES, STIFFLY
1¼	TBSP FLOUR		BEATEN
5	EGG YOLKS, WELL	1	9-INCH BAKED
	BEATEN		PIE SHELL
1	TBSP UNFLAVORED	1	C HEAVY CREAM,
	GELATIN		WHIPPED
2	TBSP COLD WATER		GRATED MILK
½	TSP NUTMEG		CHOCOLATE

Scald milk. Cool slightly and mix into sugar and flour, which have been sifted together. Add gradually to egg yolks while beating. Cook in double boiler, stirring constantly until thick. Mix in gelatin that has been softened in cold water. Remove from fire and cool.

Add nutmeg and brandy, then fold in egg whites. Pour into pie shell. Chill until firm. Top with whipped cream and sprinkle with grated milk chocolate.

BUTTERSCOTCH-PECAN BRITTLE PIE

2	EGG YOLKS, WELL	2	EGG WHITES, STIFFLY
	BEATEN		BEATEN
¾	C FIRMLY PACKED	2	TBSP SUGAR
	BROWN SUGAR	2	C CRUSHED PECAN
1	C MILK, SCALDED		OR PEANUT BRITTLE
2	TBSP BUTTER	1	C HEAVY CREAM,
1	TBSP UNFLAVORED		WHIPPED
	GELATIN	1	9-INCH BAKED
¼	C COLD WATER		PIE SHELL
1	TSP VANILLA	1	TSP DARK RUM

Add brown sugar to egg yolks and beat well. Gradually mix in milk and butter. Cook in double boiler until slightly thickened. Remove from the heat. Soak gelatin in cold water and add to hot custard. Stir until dissolved. Mix in vanilla. Cool, then chill.

When mixture begins to set, fold in egg whites, to which two tablespoons of sugar have been added. Carefully mix in pecan brittle and half of the whipped cream. Pour into pie shell and top with remaining whipped cream, sweetened to taste and flavored with rum. Serves 6.

RUM BUTTERSWEET PIE

16	GINGERSNAPS, ROLLED FINE	1	TSP VANILLA
5	TBSP BUTTER, MELTED	1	TBSP UNFLAVORED GELATIN
1	C PLUS 2 TBSP SUGAR	¼	C COLD WATER
1¼	TBSP CORNSTARCH	4	EGG WHITES
4	EGG YOLKS, WELL BEATEN	¼	TSP CREAM OF TARTAR
2	C MILK, SCALDED	2	TBSP RUM
1½	SQ UNSWEETENED CHOCOLATE, MELTED	1	C HEAVY CREAM, WHIPPED

Line a 9-inch pie pan with gingersnaps and butter that have been combined. Bake at 350°F for 10 minutes. Cool.

Mix ½ cup of the sugar and cornstarch together. Beat into egg yolks. Gradually add milk, while stirring. Cook over boiling water for 20 minutes, stirring constantly. To 1 cup of this custard add chocolate and vanilla. Cool, pour into crust, and chill.

Soak gelatin in water. Stir into remaining hot custard. Cool. Sprinkle egg whites with cream of tartar. Beat until stiff. Gradually add remaining ½ cup sugar and beat well. Just before gelatin mixture sets, fold in meringue and rum. Spread carefully over chocolate pie. Chill until set.

Top with whipped cream, to which 2 tablespoons sugar has been added. Sprinkle with grated bitter chocolate, if desired.

OSGOOD PIE

1	9-INCH PIECRUST	1	TBSP NUTMEG AND CINNAMON COMBINED
1	C PECANS		
1½	C SUGAR		
1	C RAISINS	4	EGG WHITES, STIFFLY BEATEN
4	EGG YOLKS		

Bake piecrust. Heat pecans, sugar, raisins, egg yolks, and spices until sugar is melted; then add egg whites. Pour mixture into piecrust and bake at 300°F until brown, 35 to 45 minutes. Serve with whipped cream if desired.

LEMON PIE

1¼	C SUGAR	3	EGG YOLKS, WELL BEATEN
¼	TSP SALT	½	C (SCANT) LEMON JUICE
6	TBSP CORNSTARCH GRATED RIND OF 1 LEMON	1	10-INCH BAKED PIE SHELL
2	C BOILING WATER	3	TBSP SUGAR
4	TBSP BUTTER	3	EGG WHITES

Combine sugar, salt, cornstarch, and grated rind. Add water slowly. Simmer over a low flame until clear and thick, stirring constantly. Cover and cook over boiling water for 10 minutes more. Add butter.

Mix egg yolks and lemon juice together. Gradually pour in hot mixture and beat well. Place in pie shell and bake at 400°F for 10 minutes. Add 3 tablespoons sugar to egg whites and beat until very stiff. Cover pie with this meringue and bake again at 350°F until lightly browned.

CHOCOLATE CHUNK-PECAN PIE

9	EGGS	½	C CHOCOLATE CHUNKS
2	C DARK BROWN SUGAR	½	C PECAN PIECES
3	C DARK CORN SYRUP	3	UNBAKED 9-INCH DEEP-DISH PIE SHELLS
1	C BUTTER, MELTED		

Preheat oven to 350°F. In mixing bowl combine eggs, brown sugar, corn syrup, and melted butter. Mix until well blended; set aside. Put chocolate chunks and pecan pieces equally into bottoms of three unbaked pie shells. Measure out 2 cups eggs mixture per pie and pour over the pecan pieces and chocolate chunks. Bake for 25 minutes or until golden brown. Makes 3 pies. Serves 24.

PUMPKIN CHIFFON PIE

1½	C COOKED PUMPKIN	1	TSP GRATED
3	EGG YOLKS, SLIGHTLY		ORANGE RIND
	BEATEN	1	TBSP UNFLAVORED
½	C HALF-AND-HALF		GELATIN
½	TSP SALT	¼	C COLD WATER
½	TSP GINGER	1	C FIRMLY PACKED
¾	TSP CINNAMON		BROWN SUGAR
		3	EGG WHITES

Heat pumpkin in double boiler for 10 minutes. Mix egg yolks with half-and-half, salt, ginger, and cinnamon. Add to pumpkin and cook until of custard consistency. Remove from heat and add orange rind. Stir in gelatin that has been soaked in cold water for 5 minutes until dissolved. Chill.

Add brown sugar gradually to egg whites and beat until very stiff. When gelatin mixture begins to set, fold in this meringue. Pour into a 9-inch cooked pastry shell, or the following graham cracker crust. Chill until firm.

GRAHAM CRACKER CRUST

¾	C GRAHAM CRACKER	2	TBSP BUTTER,
	CRUMBS		MELTED
¼	C SUGAR	1½	TSP WATER

Combine sugar, crumbs, and butter. Add water and mix well. Press firmly into the sides and bottom of a 9-inch pie pan. Bake at 400°F for 10 minutes. Cool. Chill and fill.

APPLE PANDOWDY

4	MEDIUM-SIZE TART APPLES, PEELED AND THINLY SLICED	½	TSP CINNAMON
		¼	TSP SALT
		¼	C MOLASSES
½	C SUGAR	½	C WATER

Place apple slices in the bottom of a greased, shallow baking dish. Sprinkle with combined sugar, cinnamon, and salt. Mix molasses and water together and pour over all. Top with the following pastry.

PASTRY

1	C SIFTED FLOUR	⅓	C SHORTENING
1½	TSP BAKING POWDER	⅓	C MILK
¼	TSP SALT		

Sift flour, baking powder, and salt together. Cut in shortening. Add milk and mix thoroughly. Roll ⅓-inch thick and lay over apples. Prick with a fork. Bake at 450°F for 20 to 25 minutes. Serves 8.

COUNTRY FRUIT PIE

6	REFRIGERATED PIECRUSTS	9	FRESH PLUMS (ABOUT 3 C), CUT INTO SIXTHS
15	FRESH PEACHES OR NECTARINES (ABOUT 9 C), CUT INTO EIGHTHS	1	C HONEY
		9	TBSP FLOUR
		½	TSP ALMOND EXTRACT

Preheat oven to 400°F. Following package directions, unfold three piecrusts and place in three 8-inch pie dishes. In bowl, lightly toss fruit with remaining ingredients. Spoon fruit into crusts. Add top crusts and bake 25 to 30 minutes until crusts are browned and fruit is easily pierced with a knife. Makes 3 pies. Serves 24.

COUNTRY APPLE PIE

6   C COOKING APPLES,
    PEELED AND SLICED
1   TBSP LEMON JUICE
½   C FIRMLY PACKED
    BROWN SUGAR
½   C SUGAR
2   TBSP FLOUR

½   TSP GROUND
    CINNAMON
¼   TSP GROUND
    NUTMEG
2   TBSP BUTTER OR
    MARGARINE
    PASTRY FOR DOUBLE-
    CRUST 9-INCH PIE

Roll half of pastry to ⅛-inch thickness on a lightly floured surface. Place in a 9-inch pie plate; set aside. Combine apples and lemon juice in a large mixing bowl. Combine sugars, flour, cinnamon, and nutmeg, mixing well. Spoon over apple mixture, tossing gently. Spoon filling evenly into pastry shell and dot with butter. Roll remaining pastry to ⅛-inch thickness; transfer to top of pie. Trim off excess pastry along edges. Fold edges under and flute. Cut slits in top crust for steam to escape. Cover edges of pastry with strips of aluminum foil to prevent excessive browning. Bake at 450°F for 15 minutes. Reduce heat to 350°F and bake for an additional 35 minutes. Makes one 9-inch pie.

SOUTHERN MANSION MOLASSES PIE

5   EGG YOLKS, WELL
    BEATEN
2   C SUGAR
1   HEAPING TBSP FLOUR
1   C MOLASSES
1   C CREAM
1   TBSP SOFTENED
    BUTTER

½   TSP CINNAMON
½   TSP CLOVES
½   TSP NUTMEG
    SALT
5   EGG WHITES
1   10-INCH UNBAKED
    PIE SHELL

Add 1½ cups of sugar and the flour gradually to egg yolks and beat until creamy. Mix in molasses, cream, butter, spices, and a pinch of salt. Pour into pie shell. Bake at 375°F for 30 to 40 minutes, or until firm.

Gradually add the remaining ½ cup sugar and a pinch of salt to egg whites, and beat well. Cover the top of pie with this meringue. Reduce oven to 300°F and bake until lightly browned.

TEXAS PECAN PIE

½   C SUGAR
1   C WHITE CORN SYRUP
3   EGGS
4   TBSP MARGARINE,
    MELTED
    DASH SALT

1   TBSP VANILLA
    EXTRACT
1   C BROKEN PECANS
1   UNBAKED 9-INCH
    PIECRUST

Cook sugar and syrup until thickened. Beat eggs; slowly add hot syrup to eggs, beating constantly. Add melted margarine, salt, vanilla, and pecans and pour into unbaked piecrust. Bake in preheated 450°F oven for 10 minutes. Lower temperature to 300°F and bake 35 minutes.

NO-SUGAR APPLE PIE

    PASTRY FOR DOUBLE-
      CRUST 9-INCH PIE
3   TBSP CORNSTARCH
1   C SUGAR SUBSTITUTE
¾   TSP GROUND
      CINNAMON
¼   TSP GROUND
      NUTMEG

¼   TSP SALT
8   CUPS GRANNY SMITH
      OR OTHER BAKING
      APPLES (ABOUT
      8 MEDIUM), SLICED,
      CORED, AND PEELED

To make crust, roll half the pastry on floured surface into circle 1 inch larger than inverted 9-inch pie pan. Ease pastry into pan.

To make filling, combine cornstarch, sugar substitute, cinnamon, nutmeg, and salt, and sprinkle over apples in large bowl and toss. Arrange apples in piecrust. Roll remaining pastry into circle large enough to fit top of pie. Place over apples. Seal edges, trim, and flute. Cut a few slits in top of pastry to allow steam to escape. Bake in preheated 400°F oven 40 to 50 minutes, or until crust is golden and apples are tender. Cool on wire rack. Serve warm or at room temperature. Makes 8 servings.

LIME PIE

1	TBSP FLOUR	2	TBSP BOILING WATER
5½	TBSP SUGAR	5	EGG WHITES
5	EGG YOLKS	2	TBSP SUGAR
	JUICE AND GRATED	1	10-INCH BAKED
	RIND OF 2 LARGE		PIE SHELL
	LIMES		

Combine flour and the 5½ tablespoons sugar. Add gradually to egg yolks, and cream until very light. Add lime juice and rind. Cook over boiling water until it is the consistency of thick cream. Remove from fire and add boiling water.

Beat egg whites with 2 tablespoons sugar until stiff. Divide in half, and fold one half into the lime mixture. Put in pie shell and top with remaining half of egg whites. Bake at 300°F to brown lightly.

PARADISE PIE

8	EGG WHITES	1	C STRAWBERRIES,
8	TBSP SUGAR		OR 1 C COOKED
¼	TSP CREAM OF		DRIED APRICOTS
	TARTAR	1	C HEAVY CREAM
1	TSP VANILLA		

Beat egg whites until stiff and dry. Beat in sugar, 1 tablespoon at a time; then add cream of tartar and vanilla. Pour into two ungreased, floured layer cake pans, spreading lightly until even. Bake at 300°F for 30 to 40 minutes. Remove from oven, and let stand in pan until cool.

Crush strawberries, or if using apricots, press them through a sieve and mix until creamy. Sweeten fruit to taste. Whip cream until very stiff and sweeten slightly. Put one layer of meringue on a serving plate and spread with part of the fruit, then a layer of whipped cream. Cover with second layer of meringue and spread with the remaining fruit. Ice top and sides with whipped cream. Serve at once. Serves 6 to 8.

YOGURT CUSTARD PLUM PIE

2	EGG YOLKS	1	BAKED 9-INCH
¼	C SUGAR		PIECRUST
1	C PLAIN NONFAT	2	C SLICED FRESH
	YOGURT		PLUMS
½	TSP ORANGE PEEL	3	TBSP SIEVED APRICOT
			PRESERVES

In medium bowl, beat egg yolks and sugar until slightly thickened. Stir in yogurt and orange peel; mix well. Pour into cooled pie shell. Bake in preheated 400°F oven 8 to 10 minutes until barely set. Chill. Arrange plums over custard; brush with apricot preserves. Serves 6.

PEACH BLUEBERRY PIE

1	C SUGAR	2	C BLUEBERRIES
3	TBSP CORNSTARCH	1	TBSP LEMON JUICE
½	TSP GROUND		DOUBLE CRUST
	CINNAMON		PASTRY FOR
4	MEDIUM PEACHES,		9-INCH PIE
	PEELED AND SLICED	1	TBSP MARGARINE

In large bowl, stir together sugar, cornstarch, and cinnamon. Add peaches, blueberries, and lemon juice. Toss to coat fruit. Line a 9-inch pie plate with half of the pastry. Fill with fruit mixture. Dot with margarine.

Roll out remaining pastry for top crust. Cut slits in pastry to permit steam to escape. Bake at 400°F for 40 minutes. Makes one 9-inch pie.

CHOCOLATE MERINGUE PIE

2	SQ UNSWEETENED CHOCOLATE		1	TBSP BUTTER
½	C FLOUR		1	TSP VANILLA
1⅓	C SUGAR		1	9-INCH BAKED PIE SHELL
2⅔	C MILK		4	EGG WHITES, WELL BEATEN
4	EGG YOLKS, SLIGHTLY BEATEN		½	C SUGAR
¼	TSP SALT			

Melt chocolate in top of double boiler. Blend in thoroughly flour that has been combined with 1 cup of sugar. Gradually mix in milk. Cook over boiling water, stirring constantly, until thick. Cover and cook for 10 minutes more.

Mix ⅓ cup sugar into egg yolks. Slowly pour in chocolate mixture while beating. Return to double boiler and cook for 5 minutes. Remove from heat and stir in salt, butter, and vanilla. Cool. Pour into the pie shell. Cover with meringue made with sugar and egg whites. Bake at 300°F for about 30 minutes, or until lightly browned. Serves 6 to 8.

C A K E S   A N D
I C I N G S

CHEESECAKE

1	PKG ZWIEBACK	6	EGG YOLKS
2	C SUGAR	1	TSP VANILLA
1	TSP CINNAMON		JUICE AND GRATED
½	C BUTTER, MELTED		RIND OF ½ LEMON
6	3-OZ PKGS CREAM	½	PT WHIPPING CREAM
	CHEESE	6	EGG WHITES
¼	C FLOUR		

Roll zwieback until very fine. Add 1 cup sugar, cinnamon, and melted butter. Mix well. Grease a springform pan with some soft butter and press zwieback mixture well on bottom and sides to form a crust. Leave a portion of the mixture to sprinkle over top after filling has been added. Cream the cheese as for making a cake. Add 1 cup sugar that has been mixed with flour. Beat yolks until light. Add vanilla and lemon juice. Whip the cream and stir in, then whip the egg whites until stiff and fold into the yolk mixture. Mix egg and cream mixture together, and place the filling in the form and sprinkle top with crumbs. Bake one hour at 325°F. Turn off heat and let set in oven one hour, or until cold.

YELLOW ANGEL FOOD CAKE

5	EGG YOLKS, WELL BEATEN	½	TSP BAKING POWDER
½	C COLD WATER	½	TSP SALT
1½	C SIFTED SUGAR	5	EGG WHITES
1	TSP VANILLA	¾	TSP CREAM OF TARTAR
1½	C SIFTED CAKE FLOUR		

Pour water gradually into egg yolks and beat well. Slowly add sugar and mix thoroughly. Blend in vanilla. Sift flour, baking powder, and salt together three times, and fold into batter.

Whip egg whites until foamy with a wire whisk. Sprinkle cream of tartar over them and continue to beat until stiff but not dry. Fold gently into egg yolk mixture. Pour into a large ungreased tube pan. Bake at 300°F for 15 minutes, increase heat to 350°F, and continue to cook for 45 minutes more. Remove from oven and invert cake until cool. Frost with the following.

FROSTING

2	TSP BUTTER	ORANGE OR LEMON JUICE
2	C POWDERED SUGAR	

Cream butter and add sugar. Moisten to taste and to spreading consistency with orange or lemon juice.

CHOCOLATE ANGEL FOOD CAKE

¾	C SIFTED CAKE FLOUR	½	TSP SALT
¼	C COCOA	1¼	TSP CREAM OF TARTAR
1½	C SIFTED SUGAR		
12	EGG WHITES, STIFFLY BEATEN	1¼	TSP VANILLA

Sift flour and cocoa together seven times. Add sugar. Mix salt and cream of tartar into egg whites. Gradually fold into dry ingredients. Stir in vanilla. Pour into an ungreased tube pan. Bake at 325°F for 1 hour, or until done.

EASY CHOCOLATE CAKE

¼	C BUTTER	1	C SIFTED CAKE FLOUR
2	SQ UNSWEETENED	½	TSP BAKING SODA
	CHOCOLATE	1	TSP CREAM OF
2	EGGS		TARTAR
1	C SUGAR	1	TSP VANILLA
½	C MILK		

Melt butter and chocolate together in a double boiler. Combine eggs, sugar, milk, flour, baking soda, cream of tartar, and vanilla. Add butter-chocolate mixture. Beat with a rotary beater until well mixed. Bake in a greased 8 x 8 inch pan at 350°F for 20 to 35 minutes.

SOUR CHERRY FUDGE CAKE

8	OZ SEMISWEET	6	LARGE EGGS,
	CHOCOLATE		SEPARATED
4	OZ UNSWEETENED	1	C FLOUR
	CHOCOLATE	2	C CANNED OR
¼	C WATER		FROZEN SOUR RED
1	C UNSALTED BUTTER		CHERRIES, DRAINED
2	C SUGAR		WELL AND PATTED
2	TSP VANILLA EXTRACT		DRY WITH A
			PAPER TOWEL

Preheat oven to 300°F. Lightly grease the bottom of a 9-inch spring-form pan. Melt both chocolates with the water in the top of a double boiler placed over simmering water. Set aside to cool. Cream the butter, 1½ cups of sugar, and vanilla with mixer until light and fluffy.

Using a whisk, stir the egg yolks into chocolate mixture and add this to the butter mixture. Beat until smooth. Add flour and mix until incorporated. Beat egg whites in another bowl until frothy. Gradually add remaining ½ cup sugar and continue beating until the whites form soft peaks. Whisk one-third of the whites into the chocolate to loosen and then fold the remaining egg whites into the batter. Fold in the cherries. Pour batter into the prepared pan. Bake until it has risen and set and a tester comes out with moist crumbs (about 2 hours and 10 minutes). Cool. Makes 1 (9-inch) cake.

DEVIL'S FOOD CAKE

½	C COCOA, SIFTED	2¾	C SIFTED CAKE FLOUR
2	C SUGAR	2	TSP BAKING SODA
2	C BUTTERMILK	⅛	TSP SALT
¾	C BUTTER	1	TSP VANILLA
2	EGGS		

In bowl, combine cocoa and ½ cup of sugar. Add ½ cup of the buttermilk slowly and mix until smooth. In another bowl, cream butter with the remaining sugar, and beat until light and fluffy. Add eggs to butter and sugar, one at a time, beating well after each addition. In another bowl, sift flour, baking soda, and salt together three times. Add to butter mixture alternately with remaining buttermilk, in about three parts. Beat after each addition until smooth. Add vanilla, then cocoa mixture.

Bake at 375°F 25 to 35 minutes in two greased 8 x 8 inch pans. This cake keeps fresh and moist for a long time.

DEVIL'S FOOD CHIFFON CAKE

1	C SHORTENING	1	TSP SODA
2	C SUGAR	½	TSP SALT
2	TBSP COCOA	1	C BUTTERMILK
4	EGGS	1	TSP VANILLA
2½	C SIFTED FLOUR		

Cream shortening, add sugar, then cocoa, gradually, and mix until very light. Add eggs one at a time, beating well after each addition. Sift flour, soda, and salt together three times. Add to batter in small amounts, alternately with buttermilk. Stir in vanilla. Pour into three greased and floured 9-inch cake pans. Bake at 350°F for 35 minutes, or until done.

SOUR CREAM CUPCAKES

3	EGGS, WELL BEATEN	½	TSP BAKING SODA
1	C SUGAR	2	TSP BAKING POWDER
1	C SOUR CREAM	1	TSP VANILLA
1¾	C CAKE FLOUR		

Add sugar gradually to eggs, then sour cream. Beat well. Sift flour once, measure and sift three times with baking soda and baking powder. Add to batter and beat well. Add vanilla. Bake in paper cupcake cups placed in muffin tins, at 375°F, 15–20 minutes. Makes 24 small cakes.

Frost with orange butter icing. These are better the day after baking. Wait to ice until just before serving.

ORANGE BUTTER ICING

1½	C POWDERED SUGAR, SIFTED	GRATED RIND OF 1 LARGE NAVEL ORANGE
2	TBSP SOFT BUTTER	
2	TBSP ORANGE JUICE	

Mix all ingredients well, using enough orange juice to make icing of spreading consistency (this takes a little less than 2 tablespoons). This will frost the tops of 24 small cupcakes. Grated lemon rind and lemon juice may be substituted for the orange juice and rind.

GINGERBREAD

5	TBSP SHORTENING	1	TSP GINGER
½	C SUGAR	1	TSP CINNAMON
1	EGG, WELL BEATEN	¼	TBSP SALT
½	C DARK MOLASSES	1	TSP BAKING SODA
1¾	C SIFTED FLOUR	½	C BUTTERMILK

Cream shortening, add sugar gradually, and mix together until light. Add egg and beat well. Stir in molasses. Sift flour, ginger, cinnamon, and salt together. Add to batter, alternately with buttermilk, in which soda has been dissolved. Beat well after each addition. Pour into a greased 7 x 10 inch pan. Bake at 350°F for 25 to 35 minutes. Serves 6 to 8.

YANKEE GINGERBREAD

3	EGGS	1	C SALAD OIL
1	C SUGAR	2	TSP BAKING SODA,
1	C DARK MOLASSES		DISSOLVED IN 2 TBSP
¾	TSP CLOVES		HOT WATER
2	TSP GINGER	2	C SIFTED FLOUR
2	TSP CINNAMON	1	C BOILING WATER

Combine eggs, sugar, molasses, spices, and salad oil, and beat well. Add soda and hot water. Gradually sift in flour. Mix thoroughly. Stir in boiling water. Place in a greased 9 x 9 inch pan. Bake at 350°F for 45 minutes, or until done. Serve hot.

POUND CAKE

1	C BUTTER	1	C MILK
2	C SUGAR	1	TSP LEMON EXTRACT
6	EGG YOLKS, WELL	1	TSP ALMOND
	BEATEN		EXTRACT
3	C SIFTED CAKE FLOUR	6	EGG WHITES, STIFFLY
1	HEAPING TSP BAKING		BEATEN
	POWDER		

Cream butter, add sugar gradually, and beat well. Mix in egg yolks. Sift flour and baking powder together three times and add to batter, alternately with milk. Stir in flavorings. Fold in egg whites. Pour into a large greased tube pan. Bake at 300°F for 20 minutes.

CHOCOLATE CHIP–DATE COFFEE CAKE

STEP 1

1	C CHOPPED PITTED DATES	1½	CUPS BOILING WATER
		1	TSP BAKING SODA

Mix together and let cool.

STEP 2

½	C MARGARINE	1	TSP VANILLA EXTRACT
1	C SUGAR	1½	C FLOUR
2	EGGS	½	TSP BAKING SODA

Cream margarine and sugar together. Add eggs and vanilla. Add flour and soda. Then add all the ingredients in Step 2 to the cooled date mixture and mix well. Pour into greased and floured 9 x 13 inch pan. Sprinkle ingredients in Step 3 over top and bake 35 to 40 minutes at 350°F. May be topped with ice cream or whipped cream and served as a dessert.

STEP 3

½	C BROWN SUGAR	1	C CHOCOLATE CHIPS
½	C CHOPPED NUTS		

Mix together.

TUXPAN SPONGE CAKE

4	EGGS	4	TSP BAKING POWDER
2	C SUGAR	1	C MILK, SCALDED
3	C SIFTED CAKE FLOUR	1	TSP VANILLA

Combine eggs and sugar. Beat until very light. Sift flour and baking powder together three times and add gradually to egg mixture. Mix in milk and vanilla. Beat for 3 minutes.

Pour into an ungreased 9-inch tube pan that has wax paper on the bottom. Bake at 325°F for 50 to 60 minutes, or until done. Invert on wire rack and let stand until cool.

SWEDISH APPLESAUCE CAKE

½	C BUTTER	1½	C UNSWEETENED
1	C SUGAR		APPLESAUCE
1	EGG, WELL BEATEN	1	TSP VANILLA
2	C SIFTED FLOUR	1	C RAISINS
2	TSP BAKING SODA	1	C CURRANTS
½	TSP CINNAMON	1	C FINELY CHOPPED
¼	TSP CLOVES		PITTED DATES
		1	C BROKEN PECANS

Cream butter, add sugar gradually, and cream together until light. Add egg and beat well. Sift flour, soda, and spices together and add to batter. Mix in remaining ingredients thoroughly. Place in a greased loaf pan. Bake at 375°F for 50 minutes. Do not overcook, as this cake burns easily.

MISSISSIPPI MUD CAKE

1	C BUTTER			SALT
½	C COCOA		1½	C CHOPPED PECANS
2	C SUGAR		1	TSP VANILLA EXTRACT
4	EGGS, SLIGHTLY BEATEN			MINIATURE MARSHMALLOWS
1½	C FLOUR			

Melt butter and cocoa together. Remove from heat. Stir in sugar and beaten eggs; mix well. Add flour, pinch of salt, nuts, and vanilla. Mix well. Spoon batter into greased and floured 13 x 9 x 2 inch pan and bake at 350°F for 35 to 45 minutes. Sprinkle marshmallows on top of hot cake. Cover with chocolate frosting. Makes 1 cake.

CHOCOLATE FROSTING

1	BOX POWDERED SUGAR		⅓	C COCOA
½	C MILK		¼	C BUTTER

Combine sugar, milk, cocoa, and butter; mix until smooth. Spread on hot cake.

CHOCOLATE-NECTARINE NO-BAKE CHEESECAKE

1	8-OZ PKG LIGHT CREAM CHEESE		¼	C SEMISWEET CHOCOLATE CHIPS OR 1 TBSP GRATED UNSWEETENED CHOCOLATE
¼	C SUGAR			
½	TSP VANILLA EXTRACT			
1	PREPARED 9-INCH CHOCOLATE CRUMB CRUST		⅔	C ORANGE MARMALADE OR GINGER PRESERVES, WARMED (FOR GLAZING)
2	LARGE FRESH CALIFORNIA NECTARINES, SLICED			

In small bowl, beat cream cheese, sugar, and vanilla until smooth. Spread over bottom of pie crust. Arrange nectarine slices on cream cheese. Sprinkle center with chocolate chips. Glaze with warmed marmalade or ginger preserves. Serves 6.

KENTUCKY BOURBON CAKE

2	C BUTTER	1	C BOURBON
2⅔	C BROWN SUGAR, SIFTED	2	WHOLE NUTMEGS, GRATED
6	EGGS	2½	C RAISINS
4	C SIFTED FLOUR	2	C BROKEN PECANS
1	TSP BAKING POWDER		

Cream butter, add sugar gradually, and work together until very light. Add eggs, one at a time, beating well after each addition. Sift flour and baking powder together and add to batter, alternately with the bourbon. Mix well. Beat in nutmeg, raisins, and pecans. Pour into a large greased tube pan. Bake at 300°F for 2 hours, 15 minutes.

WHITE MOUNTAIN CREAM ICING

1	C SUGAR	2	EGG WHITES, WELL BEATEN
⅓	C WATER		
¼	TSP CREAM OF TARTAR	1	TSP VANILLA EXTRACT

Cook sugar, water, and cream of tartar until the mixture spins a long thread or until it shows 240°F on thermometer. Pour boiling syrup gradually over the well-beaten egg whites, beating until the syrup is all poured in. Add vanilla extract for flavor. Spread on top and side of cake.

PECAN-COCONUT ICING

1	C EVAPORATED MILK	¼	C BUTTER, MELTED
⅔	C BROWN SUGAR	½	C CHOPPED PECANS
2	EGG YOLKS, SLIGHTLY BEATEN	½	C SHREDDED COCONUT

Place milk, brown sugar, egg yolks, and butter in a large pan and cook until thick. Be sure to stir to keep from burning. Add pecans and coconut. Let cool. Frost top and between layers of cake.

HOT COCONUT CAKE

¼	C BUTTER	2	TSP BAKING POWDER
1	C SUGAR	¼	TSP SALT
1	EGG	¾	C MILK
2	C SIFTED CAKE FLOUR	½	TSP VANILLA

Cream butter, add sugar gradually, and mix well. Add egg and beat until light. Sift flour, baking powder, and salt together three times. Blend into batter alternately with milk. Stir in vanilla. Pour into a greased loaf pan. Bake at 350°F for about 30 minutes, or until lightly browned. Without removing from pan spread at once with the following icing.

ICING

5	TBSP BROWN SUGAR	1	TBSP CREAM
3	TBSP BUTTER, MELTED	1	C MOIST COCONUT

Combine all ingredients in the order given. Spread on hot cake. Place under broiler flame for a few minutes until browned. Serve warm.

FUDGE FROSTING

2	SQ UNSWEETENED CHOCOLATE	2	TBSP LIGHT CORN SYRUP
⅔	C MILK	2	TBSP BUTTER
2	C SUGAR DASH OF SALT	1	TSP VANILLA

Cut chocolate into pieces. Add to milk and place over low flame. Cook until mixture is smooth and blended, stirring constantly. Add sugar, salt, and corn syrup. Stir until sugar is dissolved and mixture boils. Continue cooking, without stirring, until a small amount of mixture forms a soft ball in cold water. Remove from fire. Add butter and vanilla. Cool to lukewarm. Beat until spreading consistency. Covers two 9-inch layers.

MOCHA ICING

½ C BUTTER
2 C POWDERED SUGAR
2 TBSP COCOA
2 TBSP STRONG
　 BREWED COFFEE

1 TSP VANILLA
1 C FINELY CHOPPED
　 NUTS

Cream butter. Blend in sugar, cocoa, coffee, vanilla, and nuts.

NEVER-FAIL FLUFFY ICING

2 EGG WHITES
1 C SUGAR
2 TBSP LIGHT
　 CORN SYRUP

¼ TSP CREAM OF
　 TARTAR
¼ TSP SALT
⅓ C BOILING WATER
1 TSP VANILLA

Combine all ingredients, except vanilla, in the top of a double boiler and place over rapidly boiling water. Beat with an electric mixer at high speed for 4 to 5 minutes, or just until icing will stand in peaks; or beat by hand with a rotary beater for 5 minutes, then turn off flame and continue to beat for 5 minutes more. Mix in vanilla.

This amount of icing will cover the top and sides of an 8 x 8 inch two-layer cake.

QUICK ICING FOR CUPCAKES

6 TBSP BUTTER
9 TBSP BROWN SUGAR

½ TSP VANILLA
½ C CHOPPED NUTS

Cream butter, add brown sugar gradually, and beat well. Mix in vanilla and nuts. Spread on cupcakes. Place under the broiler flame for about 1 minute, or just long enough to glaze. Serve immediately. Frosts 6 cupcakes.

SEVEN-MINUTE FOOLPROOF ICING

3	EGG WHITES	¾	C SUGAR
¾	C LIGHT CORN SYRUP	1½	TBSP WATER

Combine all ingredients in top of the double boiler. Cook over rapidly boiling water while beating with a hand or electric beater. After 5 to 7 minutes, when icing will stand in peaks, remove from the fire. This will ice an average-size layer cake, serving 12.

ICING FOR WHITE CAKE

1	C WATER	⅛	TSP CREAM OF
2	C SUGAR		TARTAR
2	EGG WHITES	1	TSP VANILLA
⅛	TSP SALT		

Boil water and sugar until the syrup forms a soft ball when dropped into cold water. Whip egg whites until frothy, and add salt. Add syrup in a thin stream. Whip constantly. When whipped, add cream of tartar and vanilla.

CRUMB CAKE

2	C FIRMLY PACKED BROWN SUGAR	¼	TSP SALT
		1	TSP SODA
1	C SIFTED BREAD FLOUR	1	TSP CINNAMON
		½	TSP CLOVES
1	C SIFTED CAKE FLOUR	1	C SOUR MILK
½	C SHORTENING	1	TSP VANILLA
1	EGG	½	TSP LEMON EXTRACT

Cut sugar and flour into shortening until it forms a crumbly mixture. Set aside 1 cup of this. To the remaining crumbs add the other ingredients. Beat for 2 minutes. Pour into a 9 x 9 inch greased cake pan. Lightly spread the reserved crumbs on top. Bake at 350°F, 45 to 50 minutes, or until done. Serve in squares. Do not attempt to remove the whole cake from pan.

C O O K I E S

BUTTERSCOTCH SQUARES

¼ C BUTTER	1 EGG
1 C FIRMLY PACKED BROWN SUGAR	¾ C SIFTED FLOUR
	PINCH OF SALT

Melt butter and brown sugar together. Remove from fire and beat in egg. Mix in flour and salt. Pour into a greased 8 x 8 inch pan. Bake at 325°F for 25 minutes; cool and cut in squares. Makes about 1½ dozen. Nuts may be added, if desired.

MAPLE-PEANUT COOKIES

⅓ C MAPLE SYRUP	⅓ C PEANUT BUTTER
½ C FIRMLY PACKED BROWN SUGAR	1¾ C FLOUR
	½ TSP BAKING SODA
1 EGG	½ TSP SALT
⅔ C SHORTENING	¼ TSP BAKING POWDER

Mix syrup, sugar, egg, shortening, and peanut butter together in a large bowl. Stir in the dry ingredients. Combine well and chill for 1 hour. Roll into balls and flatten with a fork. Bake for 8 to 10 minutes at 375°F.

QUICK BROWNIES

2	EGGS	½	C BUTTER
⅛	TSP SALT	1	TSP VANILLA
1	C GRANULATED SUGAR	½	C FLOUR, SIFTED
2	SQ UNSWEETENED CHOCOLATE	1	C COARSELY CHOPPED PECANS

Beat eggs, to which salt has been added, until thick and lemon colored. Add sugar gradually and beat well. Melt chocolate and butter together, and add to egg mixture. Add vanilla, flour, and pecans. Combine well.

Pour into a greased 7 x 7 inch pan and bake at 350°F for 20 to 25 minutes. Cut into squares while still warm. Do not overbake, as they are best if a little moist inside.

CRANBERRY COOKIES

½	C BUTTER	3	C FLOUR
1	C SUGAR	1	TSP BAKING POWDER
¾	C FIRMLY PACKED BROWN SUGAR	¼	TSP BAKING SODA
¼	C MILK	½	TSP SALT
2	TBSP ORANGE JUICE	1	C CHOPPED NUTS
1	EGG	2½	C CHOPPED FRESH CRANBERRIES

Cream butter and sugars. Beat in milk, orange juice, and egg. Sift together flour, baking powder, soda, and salt. Combine with creamed mixture and blend well. Stir in nuts and cranberries. Drop by teaspoonfuls onto a greased cookie sheet. Bake at 375°F for 10 to 15 minutes. Makes 12 dozen. Note: These cookies do not brown but will be pretty and good!

OATMEAL COOKIES

3	EGGS, WELL BEATEN	2½	C FLOUR
1	C RAISINS	1	TSP SALT
1	TSP VANILLA EXTRACT	1	TSP GROUND
1	C BUTTER		CINNAMON
1	C FIRMLY PACKED	1	TSP BAKING SODA
	BROWN SUGAR	2	C UNCOOKED
1	C SUGAR		OATMEAL

Combine eggs, raisins, and vanilla; cover with plastic wrap and let stand for one hour. Cream together butter and sugars. Add flour, salt, cinnamon, and soda to sugar mixture; mix well. Blend in egg-raisin mixture and oatmeal. Dough will be stiff. Drop by heaping teaspoonfuls onto ungreased cookie sheet or roll into small balls and flatten slightly on cookie sheet. Bake at 350°F for 10 to 12 minutes or until lightly brown.

DATE BARS

3	EGG YOLKS, WELL BEATEN	1	LB PITTED DATES, FINELY CHOPPED
1	C SUGAR	1	C BROKEN PECANS
1	C FLOUR	3	EGG WHITES, STIFFLY BEATEN
1	TSP BAKING POWDER		
¼	TSP SALT		

Add sugar to egg yolks and mix until creamy. Sift flour, baking powder, and salt together, and add dates and nuts. Blend into egg yolk mixture. You may have to knead with your fingers as it makes a stiff batter. Fold egg whites in. Smooth into a shallow 8 x 16 inch pan and bake in a 300°F oven for 30 minutes. When cool, cut into long fingers and roll in powdered sugar. Makes 25 to 30.

CHOCOLATE DROP COOKIES

1	EGG, WELL BEATEN	½	TSP BAKING SODA,
½	C FIRMLY PACKED		DISSOLVED IN
	BROWN SUGAR		½ C SOUR MILK
1⅔	C SIFTED FLOUR	2	SQ UNSWEETENED
½	TSP SALT		CHOCOLATE, MELTED
		1	TSP VANILLA
		½	C BROKEN NUTS

Gradually add sugar to egg and beat well. Sift flour and salt together and blend in, alternately, with sour milk. Beat in chocolate, vanilla, and nuts. Drop from the end of a teaspoon onto a greased cookie sheet. Bake at 350°F for 12 to 14 minutes. Makes 40 small cookies. While still warm, frost with the following icing.

ICING

1½	C SIFTED POWDERED	2	TBSP COCOA
	SUGAR	2	TBSP CREAM
2	TBSP BUTTER,		
	MELTED		

Combine all ingredients and beat until blended.

CHOCOLATE ICING FOR BROWNIES

1	TBSP BUTTER	2	TBSP MILK
¾	C POWDERED SUGAR	½	TSP VANILLA
1	HEAPING TBSP COCOA		

Cream butter. Add sugar and cocoa. Mix in milk and vanilla, beating until smooth. Spread over brownies before cutting them into squares.

COWBOY COOKIES

1	C SOFT SHORTENING OR MARGARINE	½	TSP SALT
¾	C FIRMLY PACKED BROWN SUGAR	1½	C UNCOOKED QUICK OATS
¾	C SUGAR	½	C COARSELY CHOPPED NUTS OR WHEAT GERM
2	EGGS		
1	TSP VANILLA EXTRACT	6	OZ CHOCOLATE CHIPS
2	C FLOUR		
½	TSP BAKING SODA	1	C RAISINS

Cream shortening, add sugars, and beat well. Add eggs and vanilla; stir to blend well. Add flour, baking soda, and salt at one time. Mix to blend thoroughly. Last, stir in oatmeal, nuts, chocolate chips, and raisins. Mix well. Drop by spoonfuls onto cookie sheet and bake for 13 to 15 minutes in 350°F oven. Makes 4 dozen large cookies.

This dough freezes well and can be sliced later to make fresh cookies.

HEALTHY-STYLE PEANUT BUTTER OATMEAL COOKIES

1	C FLOUR	⅓	C SUGAR
½	TSP BAKING SODA	⅓	C FIRMLY PACKED BROWN SUGAR
½	C CORN SYRUP		
½	C NATURAL PEANUT BUTTER	½	TSP VANILLA EXTRACT
		1	C UNCOOKED OATS
2	EGG WHITES		

Combine flour and baking soda and set aside. Combine corn syrup and peanut butter and mix well. Add egg whites, sugars, and vanilla. Add flour mixture and mix well. Fold in oats. Drop by rounded teaspoonfuls on ungreased cookie sheet and bake in 375°F oven for 8 minutes. Makes 2 dozen.

CHOCOLATE-ALMOND COOKIES

¼	C ALMOND OR VEGETABLE OIL	1	C CAKE FLOUR
1	C SUGAR	1	TSP BAKING POWDER
2	LARGE EGGS	¼	TSP SALT
1	TSP VANILLA EXTRACT	3	TBSP SIFTED POWDERED SUGAR
¼	TSP ALMOND EXTRACT	48	WHOLE BLANCHED ALMONDS, TOASTED*
2	SQ UNSWEETENED CHOCOLATE, MELTED AND COOLED		

B lend almond oil with sugar, eggs, vanilla, almond extract, and chocolate; mix well. Combine flour, baking powder, and salt. Blend into creamed mixture. Cover with plastic wrap and chill thoroughly several hours. Roll into 48 1-inch balls. Roll in powdered sugar; place on nonstick cookie sheet. Press almond in center of cookie. Bake at 350°F for 8 to 10 minutes. *Do not overbake.* Cool on wire rack and store in airtight container. Makes 4 dozen.

*To toast almonds, spread in ungreased baking pan. Place in 350°F oven and bake 5 to 10 minutes or until almonds are light brown; stir once or twice to ensure even browning. Note: almonds will continue to brown slightly after removing from oven.

CHEWY FUDGE SQUARES

2	EGGS, WELL BEATEN	½	C BUTTER, MELTED
1	C SUGAR	½	C SIFTED FLOUR
2	SQ UNSWEETENED CHOCOLATE, MELTED	1	TSP VANILLA
		1	C BROKEN NUTS

A dd sugar gradually to eggs, and beat well. Mix in chocolate and butter; add flour, vanilla, and nuts. Bake in a greased pan at 375°F for 30 minutes. Makes 1 dozen.

DARK SECRETS

½	C BUTTER	1½	C SIFTED FLOUR
1	C FIRMLY PACKED	½	TSP BAKING POWDER
	BROWN SUGAR	½	TSP SODA
1	EGG, WELL BEATEN	3	DROPS OLIVE OIL
¼	TSP SALT	3	SQ UNSWEETENED
½	C MILK		CHOCOLATE, MELTED
1	TSP VANILLA	1	C CHOPPED NUTS

Cream butter, add sugar gradually, and mix until light. Beat in egg, to which salt has been added. Gradually blend in milk and vanilla. Sift flour, baking powder, and soda together, and add to batter. Mix in olive oil, melted chocolate, and nuts.

Drop from teaspoon onto greased cookie sheets. Bake at 350°F for about 15 minutes, or until done. Remove from pan and ice while still hot with the following icing. Makes about 36 cookies.

ICING

1	EGG, WELL BEATEN	1	SQ UNSWEETENED
2	C POWDERED SUGAR		CHOCOLATE, MELTED
1	TSP HEAVY CREAM	1	TSP VANILLA
3	DROPS OLIVE OIL		

Add sugar gradually to egg and beat well. Mix in cream, olive oil, melted chocolate, and vanilla.

LOUISIANA WHISKEY BALLS

2½	C CRUSHED VANILLA	1	C POWDERED SUGAR
	WAFERS	3	TBSP LIGHT CORN
1	C BROKEN PECANS		SYRUP
6	TBSP WHISKEY	1½	TSP COCOA

Crush vanilla wafers and add to remaining ingredients. Mix well and form into balls. Roll in additional powdered sugar. Makes about 2 dozen small balls.

MEXICAN WEDDING FINGERS

1	C BUTTER	2	C SIFTED FLOUR
½	C POWDERED SUGAR	½	C CHOPPED NUTS

Cream butter. Add sugar, then flour, gradually. Mix well. Stir in nuts. Form into small finger shapes and place on a greased cookie sheet. Bake at 300°F for 25 to 30 minutes. Roll at once in additional powdered sugar. Makes about 4 dozen.

RUM BALLS

2	TBSP COCOA	2½	C CRUSHED VANILLA
1½	C POWDERED SUGAR		WAFERS
¼	C RUM	1	C BROKEN PECANS
2	TBSP LIGHT CORN SYRUP		

Sift cocoa and 1 cup of the powdered sugar together. Stir in rum that has been combined with corn syrup. Add wafer crumbs and pecans and mix well.

Roll into balls by the teaspoonful, and dredge in the remaining ½ cup of powdered sugar. Makes about 50.

MOLASSES CRACKLES

¾	C SHORTENING	2	TSP BAKING SODA
1	C FIRMLY PACKED BROWN SUGAR	1	TSP GROUND CINNAMON
1	EGG	½	TSP GROUND CLOVES
¼	C MOLASSES	1	TSP GROUND GINGER
1¾–2	C FLOUR	½	TSP SALT

Combine shortening, sugar, egg, and molasses; blend well. Add dry ingredients and mix. Drop by spoonfuls onto cookie sheet. Bake at 350°F for about 8 minutes. Makes 3½ dozen cookies

MOCHA CHOCOLATE CHIP COOKIES

½ C BUTTER
½ C FIRMLY PACKED
   BROWN SUGAR
½ C SUGAR
1 EGG
½ TSP VANILLA
1 C FLOUR
¼ C COCOA

2 TBSP INSTANT
   ESPRESSO POWDER
½ TSP SALT
½ TSP BAKING SODA
1½ C SEMISWEET
   CHOCOLATE CHIPS
½ C CHOPPED NUTS

Preheat oven to 350°F. Cream butter, brown sugar, and sugar until creamy. Add egg and vanilla—beat again. Sift together flour, cocoa, espresso powder, salt, and baking soda. Stir flour mixture into creamed mixture. Stir in chocolate chips and nuts. Drop teaspoonfuls onto greased cookie sheet and flatten slightly. Bake for 12 minutes. Makes 3 dozen.

APPLE-BERRY COBBLER BROWNIES

1 BOX YELLOW
   CAKE MIX
6 OZ BUTTER OR
   MARGARINE
2 BOXES FUDGE
   BROWNIE MIX

2 LBS (APPROX) GRANNY
   SMITH OR GOLDEN
   DELICIOUS APPLES
3 C (12 OZ) FROZEN
   UNSWEETENED
   RASPBERRIES
   OR BLACKBERRIES,
   THAWED

Cut butter into cake mix until the size of small peas. Keep refrigerated. Prepare brownie mix according to directions. Spread brownie batter into bottom of spray-coated 9 x 13 inch pan. Bake at 350°F for 20 minutes. Remove pan from oven. Core, peel, and chop or shred apples. Portion apples and berries over brownie batter. Top pan with cake mixture. Continue baking 30 to 40 minutes until cake top is golden brown and center is set. Cool at least 1 hour before cutting pan. Makes 35 brownies.

ICEBOX COOKIES

1	C BUTTER	½	TSP BAKING SODA
1	TSP CINNAMON		JUICE OF ½ LEMON
¾	C SUGAR	1	TSP VANILLA
¼	C FIRMLY PACKED	1	C CHOPPED NUTS
	BROWN SUGAR	2–3	C SIFTED FLOUR
2	EGGS, WELL BEATEN		

C ream butter, add cinnamon and sugars gradually, and mix until light. Beat in eggs. Dissolve baking soda in lemon juice and add to batter, together with vanilla and nuts. Work in flour, using only enough to make dough possible to handle. Form into two long rolls. Wrap in wax paper and chill in the refrigerator overnight.

Slice rolls thin crosswise and place on greased cookie sheets. Bake at 400°F for about 8 minutes, or until lightly browned. Makes 120 cookies.

SCOTCH COOKIES

2	EGGS, WELL BEATEN	2	TSP BAKING POWDER
2	C FIRMLY PACKED	½	TSP SALT
	BROWN SUGAR	1	TSP VANILLA
¾	C BUTTER, MELTED	1	C CHOPPED PECANS
3½	C SIFTED FLOUR		

G radually add sugar to eggs while beating. Mix in melted butter, then flour that has been sifted with baking powder and salt. Add vanilla and pecans. Shape into two long rolls, adding 1 or 2 tablespoons flour, if necessary, to make handling easier. Wrap in wax paper and chill for several hours.

Cut rolls into slices ¼-inch thick. Bake on greased cookie sheets at 375°F for 10 to 12 minutes. Makes about 90 small cookies.

C A N D Y

PEANUT BRITTLE

1½	C SUGAR	¼	TSP SALT
⅔	C WATER	1	TBSP BUTTER
½	C LIGHT CORN SYRUP	1	TSP BAKING SODA
1	C RAW SHELLED PEANUTS		

Combine sugar, water, and corn syrup in a saucepan. Cook, stirring only until sugar is dissolved to the soft-ball stage (236°F). Add peanuts and salt and continue cooking to 300°F, or until a little of the mixture dropped in cold water becomes very brittle.

Remove from fire. Stir in butter and soda, only enough to mix. Turn immediately onto a greased cookie sheet. Do not scrape the pan as it may cause candy to sugar. Spread, or pull, thin. Cool, and break into pieces. Makes about 90 pieces.

PRALINES

2 C SUGAR	1 C PECANS (OR MORE,
¾ C MILK	IF DESIRED)
1 TBSP BUTTER	1 TSP VANILLA
½ TSP BAKING SODA	

Combine sugar, milk, butter, and soda in a large saucepan. Cook slowly, stirring constantly until mixture reaches 238°F, or until a drop or two in cold water forms a firm ball. Remove from fire and beat. Add pecans and vanilla. Continue to beat until creamy. Drop by spoonfuls onto waxed paper that has been lightly sprinkled with salt. Makes 1½ dozen medium-size pralines.

CARAMELS

2 C SUGAR	1 C BUTTER
1¾ C LIGHT CORN SYRUP	1 TSP VANILLA
2 C HEAVY CREAM	

Combine sugar, corn syrup, 1 cup of cream, and butter in a large saucepan. Cook, stirring constantly, until boiling briskly. Gradually mix in the remaining cream. Continue to cook over low heat, while stirring, to 248°F, or until a few drops in cold water form a firm ball. Add vanilla.

Pour into greased pans. Cool, then turn out of pans uncut. Cut with a sharp knife into ¾-inch squares. Let stand for a few hours to dry, then wrap each piece in waxed paper. Makes about 2 pounds.

CREAMY MINTS

3   C SUGAR
1   C BOILING WATER
6   TBSP BUTTER

FEW DROPS
PEPPERMINT OIL

Combine sugar and boiling water and stir until dissolved. Add butter and again bring to a boil, then strain into another pan. Cover tightly and cook quickly, without stirring, to the soft-ball stage (238°F). Pour onto a marble slab, or a greased enamel tabletop or platter, without scraping the pan. Cool thoroughly.

Add oil of peppermint and stir candy with fork, working from the edges to the center. When mixture begins to get creamy, knead with the hands until stiff. Cover with damp cloth and let stand for 10 minutes.

Break off small amounts at a time, leaving the remainder covered, and cut and shape into little pieces. Wrap each portion in wax paper and store in an airtight container overnight before using. Makes about 30 small mints.

TOFFEE

1   C SUGAR
1   C BUTTER
½   LB CHOCOLATE
    SQUARES, GRATED

1½   C FINELY CHOPPED
     PECANS

Combine sugar and butter in an iron skillet. Heat over a low flame, stirring occasionally, until brown. Pour onto a well-greased platter. Sprinkle with half the chocolate. Cover with half the nuts and press them into the chocolate. Cool in the refrigerator.

Loosen candy from pan and turn over. Sprinkle with the remaining chocolate and press in the rest of the nuts. Let dry well, then break into pieces. Makes about 40 1 x 1½ inch pieces

GRAPEFRUIT PEEL

GRAPEFRUIT PEEL   SUGAR

R emove pulp and white membrane from grapefruit peel. Cut peel in
long strips ½ inch wide. Cover with water and soak for 24 hours,
changing the water several times.

Cover peel with fresh cold and water and bring to a boil. Cook for
5 minutes, drain, and repeat twice more. The third time cook until fruit
can be pierced with fork. Drain again.

Make a heavy syrup, allowing 2 cups sugar and 2 cups water for each
grapefruit. Cook to 238°F, or until a few drops in cold water form a soft
ball. Add grapefruit peel and simmer for about 10 minutes, or until most
of the water has evaporated. Shake the pan as the syrup diminishes to
prevent burning. Drain in a sieve. Roll the peel, a few pieces at a time,
in sugar. Cool and store in a covered container.

DIVINITY

3	C SUGAR	2	EGG WHITES, STIFFLY
¾	C LIGHT CORN SYRUP		BEATEN
½	C WATER	1	TSP VANILLA
		1	C CHOPPED PECANS

M ix sugar, corn syrup, and water together. Cook over a low flame,
without stirring, to a hard-ball stage (265°F). Slowly add syrup to
egg whites, while beating constantly. Add vanilla and continue to beat
until mixture will hold its shape. Add pecans, if desired. Drop from a
teaspoon onto waxed paper, or pour into a greased 8 x 8 inch pan.

SPICED NUTS

1 C SUGAR	¼ TSP CLOVES
½ TSP SALT	¼ C WATER
2 TSP CINNAMON	2¼ C NUTS
¼ TSP NUTMEG	

Combine sugar, salt, spices, and water. Cook to the soft-ball stage (238°F). Remove from fire and add nuts. Stir until it sugars. Pour onto waxed paper and separate nuts. Makes ½ pound.

SUGARED PECANS

1½ C SUGAR	GRATED RIND OF
¾ C WATER	1 ORANGE
	2 C PECANS

Combine sugar and water. Cook until syrup forms a soft ball in cold water (238°F). Remove from fire and quickly mix in orange rind and nuts. Pour onto waxed paper. When cool, break into pieces. Makes about 1¾ pounds.

CREAMY FUDGE DROPS

2 C SUGAR	2 SQ UNSWEETENED
⅔ C MILK	CHOCOLATE, FINELY
2 TBSP LIGHT	CHOPPED
CORN SYRUP	2 TBSP BUTTER
	1 TSP VANILLA
	1 C CHOPPED NUTS

Combine sugar, milk, and syrup. Bring to a boil. Add chocolate and cook stirring constantly to a soft-ball stage (238°F). Remove from fire, mix in butter, and beat until slightly cooled. Add vanilla and nuts. Beat again until a small amount dropped from a spoon will stand by itself. Working very quickly, spoon out in individual pieces onto a greased cookie sheet. Makes 2 dozen pieces.

PATIENCE

3	C SUGAR	1	C BROKEN PECANS
1	C MILK	12	OR MORE
¼	C BUTTER		MARSHMALLOWS

Combine 2 cups of the sugar, and the milk and butter in a saucepan. Cook over low heat, stirring only until sugar is dissolved.

Melt the remaining 1 cup of sugar in a skillet, without stirring, until lightly browned. Mix very gradually into the first mixture. Continue to cook to 238°F, or until a few drops in cold water form a soft ball.

Beat until candy is creamy and loses its gloss. Mix in pecans. Pour into a greased pan, the bottom of which has been covered with marshmallows. Cut into squares.

CREAMY CHOCOLATE FUDGE

2–3	TBSP BUTTER	2	TBSP MARSHMALLOW
2	C SUGAR		CRÈME
1	C EVAPORATED MILK	1	C BROKEN PECANS
	DASH SALT	1	TSP VANILLA EXTRACT
1–2	OZ CHOCOLATE		
	CHIPS		

Put butter, sugar, milk, and salt in a pan and bring to a boil. Cook gently to 236°F on candy thermometer. Stir constantly. Remove from heat and add chocolate chips and marshmallow crème. Stir until smooth. Add pecans and vanilla extract. Pour into buttered pans. Makes about 1¼ pounds of delicious fudge.

ENGLISH TOFFEE

1	C CRUSHED VANILLA WAFERS	1	C HEAVY CREAM, WHIPPED
1	C CHOPPED WALNUTS	1½	SQ UNSWEETENED CHOCOLATE, MELTED
½	C BUTTER	½	TSP VANILLA EXTRACT
1	C POWDERED SUGAR		
3	EGGS, SEPARATED		

Mix crushed wafers and chopped nuts. Spread one-half of mixture over bottom of buttered 9 x 9 inch pan. Cream butter and sugar. Add beaten egg yolks, cream, melted chocolate, and vanilla. Fold in beaten egg whites. Pour over wafers and spread remaining wafers-nut mixture on top. Refrigerate overnight. When ready to serve, cut into squares.

P O T P O U R R I

APRICOT-PINEAPPLE CONSERVE

2	LBS DRIED APRICOTS	3	C SUGAR
6	C COLD WATER	1½	C CHOPPED WALNUTS
1	20-OZ CAN PINEAPPLE		

Wash apricots well and soak them overnight in cold water. Drain, reserving liquid, and cut them and the pineapple into small pieces. Add pineapple juice, sugar, and apricot liquid.

Bring mixture to a boil and cook slowly for 1½ hours, or until thick and clear. Just before removing it from the fire, mix in chopped walnuts and pour into hot sterilized jars and seal.

PEAR BUTTER

4	LBS HARD PEARS	2	TSP CINNAMON
1	C APPLE JUICE	¼	TSP GROUND CLOVES
2	C SUGAR		

Wash and core pears. Cut in eighths and blend in a blender or food processor until smooth. If you use a blender, add ⅓ cup of apple juice with each load of pears. If you use a food processor, add the apple juice when the pears are processed. Empty mixture into a saucepan. Add the spices. Cook over low heat about 45 minutes. Pour at once into sterilized jars and seal. Makes 3 pints.

CORN RELISH

12	EARS YELLOW CORN	1	BUNCH CELERY
1	QT YELLOW ONIONS	2	TBSP TURMERIC
1	QT RIPE TOMATOES	2	QTS VINEGAR
1	QT CUCUMBERS	2	TBSP MUSTARD SEED
3	GREEN BELL PEPPERS	1	SCANT CUP SUGAR
3	RED BELL PEPPERS	⅓	C SALT
6	SMALL, HOT RED PEPPERS		

Cut corn from cob. Peel onions, tomatoes, and cucumbers, and chop. Remove veins and seeds from peppers and chop fine. Discard all but the heart and tender parts of the celery and mince.

Dissolve turmeric in a little of the vinegar. Add mustard seed. Dissolve sugar and salt in the remaining vinegar. Combine all ingredients and boil for one hour. Pour into hot sterilized jars and seal. Makes 6½ pints.

BRANDIED PEACHES

PEACHES	BRANDY
SUGAR	

Wash peaches and peel them. If preferred, make a solution of 1 tablespoon soda to 1 quart water and bring to a boil. Drop peaches in, remove immediately, and wipe with a towel to remove all fuzz. Pit peaches, if desired.

Weigh fruit and measure out 1 lb sugar and 1 cup water for every 1 lb of fruit. If peaches have pits in them, allow only ½ lb sugar to every 1 lb fruit.

Boil sugar and water together for a few minutes until a syrup is formed. Drop in a few peaches at a time and cook 5 to 10 minutes, or until they can be pierced with a straw. Remove and pack in hot sterilized jars. Continue until all peaches have been cooked.

Let syrup boil until thick, putting in additional sugar if fruit has made mixture watery. Cool. Add 1 pt brandy for every 1 pt syrup (or more if desired). Stir well and pour over peaches until jars are full. Seal at once. Brandied figs or pears may be prepared the same way.

SPICED BLACK CHERRIES

BLACK CHERRIES		1	STICK CINNAMON
SUGAR		3	WHOLE CLOVES
VINEGAR		1	GINGER ROOT

Wash, stem, and pit firm black cherries. Measure them and add an equal amount of sugar and a third as much vinegar. Place in a deep kettle with a cheesecloth bag containing spices, using more if desired.

Bring to a boil and simmer for about 1 hour, or until very thick. Discard spice bag and pour cherries into hot sterilized jars. Seal at once.

NEVER-FAIL CRANBERRY JELLY

4	C CRANBERRIES	2	C SUGAR
1¼	C WATER		

Pick over and wash cranberries well. Place in a saucepan with water. Bring to a boil and cook for about 10 minutes, or until berries burst. Press through a sieve while hot. Mix in sugar and stir until dissolved. Pour into molds without any further cooking and chill until firm. About 6 servings.

PICKLED PEACHES

7	LBS PEACHES	6	C SUGAR
	WHOLE CLOVES,	1	TBSP CINNAMON
	AS NEEDED	1	TBSP WHOLE
1	QT VINEGAR		ALLSPICE

Pour boiling water over firm peaches and let stand until skins can be removed easily. Dip in cold water, peel, and weigh. Stick 4 whole cloves in each.

Combine vinegar, sugar, cinnamon, allspice, and more cloves (as desired). Bring to a boil. Drop in peaches gradually so as not to interrupt boiling. Cook for about 10 minutes, or until fruit can be pierced easily with a fork. Remove peaches from syrup and pack in hot sterilized jars. Pour in boiling syrup to fill. Seal at once. Pears may be substituted for peaches in this recipe.

PICKLED ONIONS

10	LBS SMALL PICKLING ONIONS	1	C SUGAR
	SALT	18	FRESH HOT PEPPERS
	WATER	18	TSP CELERY SEED
1	GAL WHITE VINEGAR	18	TSP MUSTARD SEED

Soak onions in 8 tablespoons of salt and 8 quarts of water for 2 hours. Drain, peel off outer skins, and soak for 48 hours in 3⅓ cups of salt and 9 quarts of water. Drain well. Heat 1 gallon white vinegar and 1 cup sugar to the boiling point. Add onions and cook for 3 minutes. Pour onions and liquid into sterile pint jars. To each jar add 1 hot pepper, 1 teaspoon celery seed, and 1 teaspoon mustard seed. Seal well. Makes 18 pints.

TOMATO AND PEPPER RELISH

8	QTS GREEN TOMATOES	1	QT SMALL ONIONS
12	RED BELL PEPPERS	3	QTS CIDER VINEGAR
12	GREEN BELL PEPPERS	5	C SUGAR
12	HOT GREEN PEPPERS	½	C SALT

Wash and rinse 12 pint preserve jars. Place in a deep kettle of cold water. Cover and bring to a boil. Boil for 20 minutes. Leave jars in water until ready to use.

Wash tomatoes, remove stems, and quarter them. Wash sweet peppers, remove seeds and fibrous portions, and quarter. Cut stems from hot peppers. Peel and quarter onions. Put all these ingredients through a food processor. Place ground vegetables in a colander and drain off liquid, discarding it.

Put vegetables in a large kettle and add 2 quarts of vinegar. Boil uncovered for 3 minutes, stirring frequently. Again drain vegetables and discard liquid. Return to kettle. Stir in the remaining 1 quart of vinegar, the sugar, and salt. Simmer for 3 minutes. Pour immediately into sterilized jars and seal. Makes 12 pints.

SWEET CORN RELISH

20	C CANNED WHOLE-KERNEL CORN	8	C CANNED TOMATOES
2	MEDIUM HEADS CABBAGE, CHOPPED	4	C BROWN SUGAR
		1	C SUGAR
8	ONIONS, PEELED AND CHOPPED	1	C FLOUR
		1	C SALT
12	RED BELL PEPPERS, CHOPPED	1	TSP TURMERIC
		2	TSP PREPARED MUSTARD
8	GREEN BELL PEPPERS, CHOPPED	4	C VINEGAR
2	C CHOPPED CELERY	2	C WATER

C ombine all ingredients in a large pan in the order given. Bring to a boil, then let simmer for 30 minutes. Seal immediately in hot, sterilized preserve jars. Makes 24 pints.

CHOW-CHOW

1	GAL GREEN TOMATOES	3	BUNCHES CELERY
3	C COARSE SALT	5	C SUGAR
12	LARGE ONIONS	4	TBSP SALT
3	MEDIUM HEADS CABBAGE	1	TSP PEPPER
		1	TSP CAYENNE PEPPER
24	GREEN BELL PEPPERS	4	TBSP MUSTARD SEED
1	HANDFUL HOT AND GREEN RED PEPPERS	4	TBSP TUMERIC
		2	TBSP ALLSPICE
12	JONATHAN APPLES	2	TBSP CINNAMON
		1	GAL VINEGAR

R emove stem from tomatoes and slice without peeling. Pour coarse salt over them and let stand overnight. Drain. Clean onions, cabbage, and sweet and hot peppers. Put through a food grinder with tomatoes. Core and peel apples and clean celery, then chop very fine. Combine all ingredients and cook for about 1 hour. Pour into hot, sterilized jars and seal. Makes 24 pints.

CUCUMBER AND ONION RELISH

13	MEDIUM CUCUMBERS	2	TBSP MUSTARD SEED
6	MEDIUM ONIONS	1	TBSP CELERY SEED
1	C SALT	3	HOT RED PEPPERS,
2	C CIDER VINEGAR		MINCED
½	C SUGAR	4	BAY LEAVES
½	C WATER		

P eel cucumbers and onions and slice very thin. Add salt and let stand in a covered crock overnight. Drain and press dry. Combine the remaining ingredients and bring to a boil. Boil for 3 minutes. Add cucumbers and onions and let come to a boil again. Cook for 2 minutes. Pour into hot sterilized jars and seal at once.

CHILI TOMATO SAUCE

12	LARGE RIPE TOMATOES	2	C VINEGAR
4	LARGE GREEN BELL PEPPERS	2	TSP SUGAR
		1½	TSP SALT
1	LARGE ONION	1½	TSP ALLSPICE
		3	TBSP CHILI POWDER

S cald, skin, and chop tomatoes. Clean green peppers and onion and chop fine. Combine all ingredients except chili powder and mix well. Cook slowly, stirring frequently, for about 3 hours, or until thick.

Halfway through cooking, stir in chili powder (optional). Pour into hot sterilized jars and seal. Makes 2 pints.

SWEET-SOUR CUCUMBER SLICES

36	MEDIUM CUCUMBERS	2	OZ WHOLE MIXED
1	C SALT		SPICES
12	C WATER	1	OZ STICK CINNAMON
1	GAL VINEGAR	1	TSP ALUM
11	C SUGAR	1	TBSP GROUND
			CLOVES

Cut unpeeled cucumbers into ⅛-inch coins. Combine salt and water, add cucumbers, and let stand overnight. Remove from brine and cover with boiling water. Drain at once and pack in hot sterilized jars.

Mix the remaining ingredients together and bring to a boil. Fill jars with this mixture and seal immediately.

GREEN-TOMATO RELISH

20	LBS GREEN TOMATOES	6	CLOVES GARLIC,
14	MEDIUM ONIONS		SLICED
1⅓	C SALT	¼	TSP CAYENNE PEPPER
2½	QTS CIDER VINEGAR	1⅓	TBSP CINNAMON
5	C SUGAR	1¼	TSP GROUND CLOVES
2⅓	TBSP MUSTARD SEED	2½	TSP CELERY SEED
1⅓	TBSP DRY MUSTARD	1¼	TSP GROUND
			ALLSPICE

Peel tomatoes and onions. Slice very thin. Place in a crockery bowl, sprinkle with salt, and let stand overnight. Wash in clear water. Drain well.

Mix the remaining ingredients, stirring until seasonings are well mixed and dissolved. Pour over tomatoes and onions. Cook slowly for 1 hour, or until tomatoes are transparent, stirring frequently. Pour into sterile jars and seal. Makes 18 pints.

ICEBOX PICKLES

6	LARGE DILL PICKLES, SLICED CROSSWISE	4	CLOVES GARLIC
3	C SUGAR	1	TSP WHOLE ALLSPICE
		4–5	BAY LEAVES

Combine all ingredients in a covered crock. Let stand at room temperature for 24 hours. Place in the refrigerator for 24 hours more. Makes about 1 pint.

SWEET CRISP PICKLES

6	SOUR PICKLES	3	TBSP PICKLING SPICES
4	HEAPING C SUGAR	3	TBSP SALAD OIL

Cut two of the pickles (do not use dill pickles) in ¼-inch coins. Place in a bowl and cover with 1 heaping cup of the sugar. Repeat until all pickles are used, adding the extra cup of sugar last.

Tie pickling spices in two cheesecloth bags and put in with the pickles. Pour in salad oil. Cover bowl with a plate and let stand in refrigerator for three days, stirring each day.

At the end of the third day, pickles are ready to use. Store covered in pint jars. It is not necessary to seal jars as for most pickles. Makes 3 pints.

PEACH BUTTER

PEACHES   SUGAR

Wash and cut up ripe, unpeeled peaches. Leave a few stones for flavor. Place in a deep kettle; add water to barely cover. Cook until soft, stirring constantly. Press through a colander, then through a fine sieve.

Measure pulp and add an equal quantity of sugar. Pour into a roasting pan. Bake, uncovered, at 350°F for 1½ to 2 hours, until thick, stirring often during cooking. Pour immediately into hot sterilized jars and seal at once.

If a tart peach butter is desired, reduce sugar one-half to one-third for every 2 cups pulp.

SUN CHERRIES

SOUR CHERRIES   SUGAR

Wash and pit sour cherries. Weigh them and add an equal amount of sugar, pound for pound. Place in a deep kettle and bring to a boil. Cook for 6 to 8 minutes, until tender, but still firm.

Pour into shallow platters and cover with glass. Place in the sun for about 2 days, or until syrup is thick. At the end of each day, stir well. Pour into hot sterilized jars and seal at once with paraffin.

WILD PLUM JELLY

PLUMS   SUGAR

Wash wild plums well, removing any stems. Add ½ cup water for 1 pound of fruit. Cook in a deep kettle in amounts not more than 8 quarts. Cook until soft and mushy. Cool until able to handle.

Working with a small amount at a time, strain juice and pulp through a colander. Work and squeeze hard until all juice is extracted. (Jelly will become clear when it is cooked.) Strain again through a very fine cloth such as a man's handkerchief.

For every 3 cups juice, add 2 cups sugar. Cook in amounts of not more than 4 cups. Stir only until sugar is dissolved. Cook, skimming when necessary, to 219°F, or until liquid falls in a sheet from a spoon. Pour into hot sterilized jars to within ½ inch of the top. Seal with paraffin.

WAKE-UP PEACH WAFFLES

2	C REDUCED-FAT ALL-PURPOSE BAKING MIX	2	TBSP OIL NONSTICK COOKING SPRAY
1⅓	C APPLE JUICE	4	FRESH PEACHES, SLICED
1	EGG		

Preheat waffle iron. In medium bowl, combine baking mix, juice, egg, and oil. Lightly coat iron with nonstick spray. Pour about ⅔ cup batter into iron. Cook according to manufacturer's instructions. Serve with peach slices. Makes 5 waffles.

WATERMELON RIND PRESERVES

4	LBS WATERMELON RIND	2	OZ GINGER
5	OZ STACK LIME*	8	C SUGAR
		2	LEMONS, SLICED

Before weighing, cut green rind away from the red meat of the watermelon. Chop rind into small pieces of uniform shape and size. Dissolve lime in 2 gallons of cold water. Soak fruit in mixture overnight. In the morning, drain and rinse well with two changes of water. Cover with fresh water and soak again for 3 hours. Drain.

Mix ginger into 1 gallon of water and add rind. Bring to a boil and cook for 20 minutes. Drain again. Stir sugar and lemon into 3 quarts fresh water, bring to a boil, add rind, and cook until clear and tender. Pour into hot sterilized jars and seal at once. Additional spices may be used, if desired.

*Also known as calcium hydroxide. Available at pharmacies.

STRAWBERRY PRESERVES

4	C STRAWBERRIES	5	C SUGAR

Wash and hull strawberries. Place in a deep heavy kettle together with sugar. Cook over a low flame, stirring constantly, until sugar melts. Turn heat high and bring it to a boil. Boil for 12 minutes. Skim during cooking.

Let stand overnight to plump the berries. Pour into hot sterilized jelly glasses to within ½ inch of the top. Cover with a layer of hot paraffin. Makes 8 to 10, 6-oz glasses. Do not cook more than this amount in one kettle.

GRAPE JELLY

CONCORD GRAPES	TART APPLES, DICED
WATER	SUGAR

U se Concord grapes (including some that are underripe). Wash, stem, and place them in a deep kettle. For every quart of grapes add ½ cup water and 1 cup diced tart apples. (The apple will prevent crystals from forming in the jelly; the flavor will not be apparent.) Simmer until grapes are tender. Strain through a jelly bag without squeezing.

For every 1 cup juice use ¾ to 1 cup sugar, depending on tartness desired. Spread sugar on shallow pans and place in a 300°F oven until hot.

Working with amounts of 4 cups, bring juice to a boil and cook rapidly for 10 minutes. Add hot sugar and continue to cook until a little will jell on a cool saucer. Skim as needed. Pour into hot sterilized glass and seal.

ORANGE MARMALADE

3	MEDIUM ORANGES	2½	QTS WATER
2	LEMONS		SUGAR

P eel oranges. Remove white membrane from inside the peelings of two of the oranges. Discard seeds. Put clean peelings and one orange pulp through the coarse blade of a food processor. Measure out 3 cups, using more oranges if necessary.

Cut lemons in half lengthwise and remove seeds. Cut into very thin slivers. Fill 1 cup, packing it firmly, using more or less lemon. Combine all fruit, add water, and let it stand overnight.

Bring mixture to a boil and cook for about 1 hour, or until peel is tender. Let it stand overnight again. Measure fruit and juice and add an equal amount of sugar, cup for cup. Mix well and cook to about 220°F, or until marmalade falls in a sheet from a spoon. Skim and pour into hot sterilized jars. Seal. Makes about 3 pints.

APPLE BUTTER

20	APPLES, UNPEELED	½	TSP NUTMEG
8	C APPLE CIDER*	¼	TSP ALLSPICE
4	C SUGAR	⅛	TSP CLOVES
2	TBSP CINNAMON		

Wash apples, quarter and core; do not peel. Combine with cider and cook until tender. Run through a sieve. Add remaining ingredients and cook 2 hours on top of stove. Then place in deep roasting pan and cook in oven at 350°F for 2 more hours. Can in sterilized jars with a paraffin seal. This is really the most delicious apple butter ever, and so easy to make. The baking is what makes it special.

*Not cider vinegar!

SUN'S-UP PANCAKES

4	FRESH NECTARINES	1	EGG, LIGHTLY BEATEN
2	C REDUCED-FAT ALL-PURPOSE BAKING MIX		NONSTICK COOKING SPRAY
1½	C ORANGE JUICE OR APPLE JUICE		

Chop 1 nectarine to make 1 cup. Slice remaining nectarines; set aside. In medium bowl, combine baking mix, juice, and egg *until just moistened*. Do not overmix. Stir in chopped fruit. Heat griddle or skillet over medium heat; coat with nonstick spray. Spoon ¼ cup batter onto griddle; spread out mixture slightly with back of spoon. Cook until bubbles form on top and underside is golden brown. Turn pancakes; cook until golden brown. Top with nectarine slices. Serves 6.

ABOUT THE AUTHOR

JAMES STROMAN is president of his own food manufacturing company and has written several cookbooks including *Country Inn Cooking*; *Prize Recipes from Great Restaurants: The Western States*; *Prize Recipes from Great Restaurants: The Southern States and the Tropics*; *The Great Country Inns of America Cookbook* (now in its third edition); *Dining Out at Home*; and *From Texas Kitchens*. He lives in Dallas, Texas.